The Samurai Samba Vinci Way

Claudio Toyama

Praise for The Samurai Samba Vinci Way™

"Claudio Toyama has written a must-read primer for anyone who has been recently promoted into a leadership role...Read this book - and learn to be global and UNSTOPPABLE from one of the best." — **Doug Bruhnke, CEO, Global Chamber.**

"In early 2015, as a recently nominated TED Fellow, I was given the opportunity to work with a coach to develop my overall professional skills. TED runs a program called SupportTED which provides different types of support to its fellows, including professional coaching. Claudio Toyama was selected as a good match for me, and we have been working together since then.

When we first spoke, we talked about what the main focus of my coaching would be and Claudio made me think REALLY hard and talk about all the different issues I deal with as a wildlife conservationist in Brazil.

My focus is mostly on animal conservation, but I also deal with human beings all the time, particularly my staff. I quickly realized that this was where I really needed Claudio's help. My program in Brazil is growing and expanding. With the addition of many staff members, managing them is becoming harder. Claudio and the Samurai Samba Vinci Way™ helped me think about things I haven't considered in the past. How do I become a good leader to my team? How do I work with the team? What are their similarities and differences? How do I identify their skills? How do I better channel their passion and commitment?

How do I encourage them to grow and become conservation leaders themselves?

Using the concepts presented here in the Samurai Samba Vinci Way™, Claudio has been incredibly helpful in making me ask and answer all these difficult questions. Most importantly, he has helped me think about different ways to manage and supervise different members of my staff. The results have been fantastic. I have been constantly impressed by Claudio's ability to guide me through this process.

I had never had a coaching experience before working with Claudio, and I have to admit I had no idea how useful and – to a certain degree – life-changing it would be. Claudio Toyama is an amazing coach. I'm thrilled he has written this book so others can benefit from his tremendous wisdom. I hope to have the opportunity to continue working with him for many years to come!" — **Patricia Medici, Wildlife Conservationist/ Ph.D. in Biodiversity Management, TED Fellow and Speaker.**

The Samurai Samba Vinci Way:

How to Improve Your Executive Presence, Increase Trust and Lead Your Team at a World-Class Level

Claudio Toyama

THE SAMURAI SAMBA VINCI WAY
How to Improve Your Executive Presence, Increase Trust and
Lead Your Team at a World-Class Level

Solsten Publishing

ISBN   13 978-0-9990103-0-3   Paperback
           10 0-9990103-0-1

ISBN   13 978-0-9990103-1-0   Kindle
           10 0-9990103-1-X

Digital editions can also be found at other online platforms
including Barnes and Noble.
For privacy purposes, some names in the book have been

changed.

Dedication

To my daughter Annika, who reminds me every single day of what joy feels like.

I am truly blessed to have you in my life.

"It's not the mountain that we conquer, but ourselves."

Sir Edmund Hillary

ACKNOWLEDGMENTS

A lot of people are behind a book, and mine is no exception. My writing coach, cheerleader and editor, Mary Lou Kayser, made this book possible for me. I couldn't have done it without her.

I also want to thank Dr. John Mather for writing the marvelous foreword, and Patricia Medici for not only saying great things about my coaching, but also for the wonderful feedback and words of encouragement.

My friend Wendy Baird and her team at Insight180 for the wonderful branding for my business and this book cover.

My family members, who have always believed in me, especially my mother Beth Toyama, my brother Fabio Toyama and sister Christina Ivanov; my grandmother Yoshie Toyama, my uncle Kosaburo Toyama, my aunt Maura Regina Ludewig; my cousins Marina and Ana Margareth. You all made me feel less inadequate as I was growing up.

My father Yoshijiro Toyama, who, in his own way, helped mold me into who I am today. His lack of acknowledgment was a driving force behind me wanting to excel in so many areas in my life. At the time, I didn't see that as a blessing; thankfully, I have come to realize how fortunate I was.

To Marin Gemmill-Toyama, for her support, in so many different ways. I really appreciated it.

My friends Alexandre Caetano, Alan Dubner, Rod Abbamonte and Thomas Ahn, who believed in me in my darkest periods.

My friends Maria Ana Botelho Neves, Stephen Barrett, and Neil Gibb, for always challenging me to think "beyond the box."

To Renee Simas, for her exceptional line editing skills.

My ex-bosses and friends, José Edson Bacellar and Shaun Smith, for pushing me towards mastery.

My work colleague and friend, Nancy Martin, for the strong belief in me.

My teachers who have had an impact on how I see the world, especially Walter (my third grade math teacher), Julio Olalla from Newfield Network and Bob Dunham, from the Institute for Generative Leadership.

All of my clients in executive coaching, leadership development, customer and employee experience consulting projects.

All the philosophers, thinkers, professors and writers who contributed to shifting my own thinking about the world we live in, including: Bob Anderson, Ken Wilbur, Peter Senge, Noam Chomsky, Naomi Klein, Richard Barrett, Dan Pink, the brothers Chip and Dan Heath, and so many others.

To all the Samurai Samba Vinci workshop attendees in the different countries I have delivered it, for your suggestions for improvement and words of encouragement.

And for the thousands of people (literally!) who have crossed my path along the way in the 40+ countries I have visited, who have taught me so much, either by your teachings, your wisdom, your informal conversations or just by your presence -- thank you!

CONTENTS

FOREWORD

Who am I today? If I "contain multitudes," as Walt Whitman said in his iconic poem, "Song of Myself," which one will speak and act for me at this moment, or an hour from now, or tomorrow?

As an astronomer working with brilliant scientists, engineers, and managers, I see how we all possess a wide diversity of thought and feeling. Some of us are visionary, some detail-oriented, while others are all about people. This array of perspectives adds luster and shine to a world that can, at times, be tarnished.

I've taken management courses on and off for years, and most were forgettable. I've learned about the Myers Briggs types, and I've participated in counseling and coaching designed to improve my skills. But I've never seen anyone talking about what Claudio Toyama presents in this book: the three personalities of the Samurai, the Samba, and the Vinci that comprise the SSV Way™ and provide an exceptional path to leadership.

Claudio has many stories to tell based on examples from his own life of trial and error and from his work as a coach developing subject matter experts into leaders. The stories are memorable, and after you read them, he asks you questions. Answer them, and see what happens next.

I've been fortunate to have experienced Claudio's personal coaching in public speaking. Claudio has a way of looking, thinking and feeling that cuts through confusion and opens doors of clarity. This book can help open doors for you, too.

In a world that seems to be full of competition, combat, and winner-take-all rewards for bad behavior, how can we sense our place and our possibilities to ask for what we really want? Is there anything really holding us back from being the leaders we are meant to be?

Maybe not. Maybe we need only to see and feel differently, to think and act differently. Maybe the Samurai, the Samba, and the Vinci within us are already there, waiting for this book to help them come out into the open and guide us toward what's next.

Mastery doesn't have to be only about struggle, hard work and determination. It can also be about perspective, understanding and "we-thinking" for leadership – and, having a little fun along the way!

I hope you will find this book inspiring and practical at the same time.

Dr. John C. Mather
Nobel Prize in Physics Laureate
Senior Astrophysicist - NASA Goddard Space Flight Center
May 2017

INTRODUCTION

I grew up in São Paulo, Brazil, about 270 miles southwest of Rio de Janeiro. Brazil is known for being laid back, but when I lived there, a military dictatorship ruled the nation. Citizens were not allowed to express themselves freely, nor were they able to criticize the government. As a child, I was unaware of the political climate or the restrictions it placed on the people of Brazil. All I knew about life came from the richness of my family, an eclectic mix of people and cultures that would form the bedrock of what I now call the Samurai Samba Vinci Way™.

My father came from a traditional Samurai and sword making family and was no stranger to hard work and study. He was of Japanese descent, a heritage known for its dedication to mastery and precision, core elements of the Samurai persona. Just like my uncles and aunts, my father "put in the hours" so that he could advance in the companies he worked for.

After losing everything in the Second World War, he and his family emigrated to Brazil when he was 16 years old. Right after the war, Brazil, Argentina, America and some other countries were open to immigration as they needed workers. The abolishment of slavery drove this need, and immigrants were thought to be a good option to handle the growing economy. He worked for many years on a plantation in the countryside of São Paulo State before the family moved to São Paulo City. At that point, my father and some of my uncles started working at a Japanese bank in the city.

Eventually, my father secured a position with the automobile industry, spending over 30 years in it and climbing the proverbial

1

"corporate ladder" to eventually retire as a financial controller of the Brazilian operations of an American company.

Unlike my father, my mother is half Italian, half Austrian, a mix that could not be more Vinci in that it favors creativity, innovation, and dreaming up new ideas. She grew up in Brazil, and started working relatively young. She eventually left her employed position to take care of the children, but she never lost her desire to continue her studies. In true Vinci fashion, she eventually finished her degree in fine arts and has since won numerous prizes for both of her passions: oil painting, and nature and bird photography.

The cultural clash between my parents couldn't have been greater and illustrated for me as a child the concepts I am now sharing in this book. My father was the only one of his siblings to marry a non-Japanese descendant. The Japanese culture is very hard-working, polite and formal. My aunts and uncles refrained from hugging and were much more "serious" and quiet when we were together. To this day, I remember my aunt extending her hand to me in greeting when I tried to hug her. As a child, I thought that was quite funny.

My mother's side of the family behaved much differently than my father's. The Italian influence was predominant, with a lot of laughter, hugging, vibrancy, and loudness. When all of that mixed into the melting pot of Brazilian culture -- which is known for its playfulness, spontaneity and love of improvisation (key characteristics of the Samba persona) -- a fascinating family dynamic existed for me, forging the foundation of what would become my life's work.

Despite being immersed in this rich, multi-faceted family, I couldn't fully appreciate any of the personas until much later in life. The way of the Samurai, for instance, was too rigid for me, even though I had internalized and developed many of its characteristics, such as the aim for mastery and the need for continuous improvement in everything that I do.

That rigidity came to life for me one night when I had a conversation with my father on the phone while I was out with my friends. It was during the time when I was preparing to enter college. In Brazil, you have to apply to each college or university that you want to get into. Each college or university has its own five-hour test that covers geography, world and Brazilian history, biology, physics, mathematics, Portuguese literature and grammar, and English.

On that particular Friday night, our plans changed from what I had originally told my parents I would be doing. I called home to let them know that I would be going to another place before coming home. In true Samurai fashion, my father said when he answered the phone, "You should be studying for your tests. Come back home immediately!"

He then hung up, leaving me talking to myself on the other end of the line. I told my friends that my father just hung up on me and demanded that I go home. They thought I was joking, and immediately started laughing. But it was not a joke. So much so that when I got home, I called forth the Samurai within me and told my father – who was waiting in the living room for me – "I will live my life the way I want to. If I don't get into college, I will follow your rules, no questions asked. If, on the other hand, I manage to get into college, you don't get any say on how I study. Deal?"

"Deal!" he replied, with a big smile on his face.

I followed through on my promise and studied hard. I also had fun while doing it and eventually was accepted into what was considered the best business administration college in Latin America at the time.

By the time I left for college, I was already a mix of the different personas. In fact, I have come to consider myself to be more of a Vinci-Samurai type of person with a side of Samba as I also love to be spontaneous; I love to enjoy life, and I am very playful. I'm not fully Samba, though, as I don't like too much chaos or too much improvisation without a plan.

On the Vinci side, I have always loved innovative ideas and the amalgamation and cross-pollination of different fields of knowledge. Maybe that's why I have formally studied business administration, marketing, communications, graphic design, interactive multimedia, coaching, executive coaching, generative leadership, numerous healing modalities and have attended conferences on several diverse topics.

The idea of the Samurai Samba Vinci Way™ came to me ten years ago, but it was not the right time yet to pursue it. More of a seed than a bushel of wheat, it needed to go through its natural cycle of planting, cultivating and harvesting before I could bring it to the world.

That cycle has been ongoing for many years as I have been teaching high performing subject matter experts and organizations around the world about effective leadership development using pieces of the Samurai Samba Vinci Way™. Participants have consistently asked me if my material was available in a book. After enough of these inquiries about my system, I decided it was time to write the book people have been asking me for.

As the speed of change continues to accelerate globally, more companies will be looking to promote internal candidates into leadership roles and train teams on effective leadership practices. Chances are good that if you are reading this book, this has happened to you. Companies can save enormous amounts of time and money when they promote internally, but only if they can also provide effective leadership training that goes beyond the superficial layers of leadership all too common in popular programs.

I initially created this book to help subject matter experts who get promoted learn how to become effective leaders for their teams and organizations. However, it became clear to me fairly quickly that the Samurai Samba Vinci Way™ can be used by anyone who is proactively seeking new insights about leadership.

In this book, I am introducing readers to what I have learned from my experience working in many different professional environments, a variety of cultures and on five different continents to shed light on how subject matter experts can increase executive presence, build more trust with their teams, and lead at a world-class level using elements of the Samurai Samba Vinci Way™ (aka: the SSV Way™).

This is by no means a "definitive" leadership book. I do not believe in a one-size-fits-all approach to leadership, and I've made no attempt to present the SSV Way™ in that fashion. Rather, my goal is to address some of the most common gaps in existing leadership development efforts, namely context, reflection, behavior change, and effective evaluation so that subject matter experts, organizational leaders, and anyone who works directly with high performers and aspires to be one can help facilitate positive and measurable change at work.

What I'm presenting here is much more than mere tools and techniques for becoming a better leader. My aim is to help shift the way we think about what a good leader is, and then provide specifics about one of the many paths we can take to effective leadership.

At its core, the Samurai Samba Vinci Way™ provides three ways for readers to become better leaders. Those ways include developing 1) a solid core and set of values through deeper self-awareness (Samurai); 2) greater flexibility, adaptability to different environments and a "go with the flow" mindset through a spirit of play (Samba); and 3) an ability to innovate and appreciate beauty through creative endeavors (Vinci). Over the years, I've come to consider myself this new kind of leader, one that draws from multiple cultures, perspectives, and traditions, who focuses as much on what's on the inside as what's on the outside to effectively lead. It took me decades to realize that the combination of the three ways of being -- while focusing on what is going on inside and outside myself -- is a fantastic mix for people who want to play and succeed at a world- class level.

You will learn that the Samurai "ethos" is about mastery and a drive for excellence and constant improvement. Samba, on the other hand, is about being flexible and adaptable to whatever life throws at you. Vinci is about amalgamating all your experience and knowledge into something that will help you and your company to move forward and be better than the competition, while better serving the stakeholders who are touched by it.

Combining these three "forces" into a new way of thinking about global leadership allows us to work with change instead of against it, opening new opportunities for ourselves and the projects we hold dear.

Indeed, the ultimate leader in the 21st century will draw on all three personas. You will start with forming a strong core and knowing what you stand for while always striving for mastery (Samurai); coupled with the ability to improvise and remain flexible and a bit more playful (i.e. not taking things too seriously) while also adapting to different situations and cultures, therefore being able to work anywhere in the world (Samba); and finally, improving your sensitivity to how different areas of knowledge intersect and being innovative (Vinci).

Most leadership books talk about the skills, methodologies, techniques and frameworks that you must first perfect to become a better leader. These are all extremely important, but what I want is for you to reflect first and foremost on who you are being when you are leading. The rest will naturally follow.

Throughout this book, I have made a conscious effort to address my readers from a gender-neutral viewpoint, using the pronouns "he," "she," and "we" interchangeably. Ultimately, this book is geared towards anyone who has or is moving into a leadership position, regardless of biological identity.

None of us can afford to play small anymore. The time to

step up and lead is now. The Samurai Samba Vinci Way™ of leadership development can help build organizations full of competent, effective and empathic leaders who inspire their teams and companies to greatness for the 21st century marketplace. We can build the companies of the future today.

I look forward to you joining me on this mission!

Claudio Toyama
Washington, D.C.
July 2017

PART I: NAVIGATING IN A NEW WORLD

Chapter 1: The World of Work Has Changed. Have You?

I will never forget the first time I went to India. I was sent there to oversee a market research project and was welcomed by my hosts, Mamata and Rajjat. I usually rent a car when I travel, but in India, I didn't dare drive for several reasons.

The first one concerns navigation. While GPS works well in big cities, it doesn't work so well in the countryside. That is not due to poor reception (even though that's the case for some parts of the country); rather, it is because many streets have no signs, and many of the roads are winding.

As Pulkit, an Indian friend once told me, directions in India are given like this:

"After you see the tree on the corner, you will see a one-eyed cow. As you pass the cow, turn right."

Of course, he was joking. But I totally know what he means.

In many countries, there are no formal rules of the road the way there are in countries like America. For instance, Brazil has lanes exclusively for turning left or right. Brazilians seldom obey these rules, however, because they know there will always be someone who will let them in. Not only that, but an unspoken rule in Brazil dictates that if you follow the rules to a T, you are considered too square and consequently, can be easily taken advantage of. This perception has been slowly changing in recent years, but I think it will take some decades to take full effect. Also, speed limits, stop signs and traffic lights are rarely acknowledged -- unless a police officer, a speed camera or a red light camera is nearby.

I have been living internationally for 22 years, and every time I go back to Brazil, my friends tell me how lucky I am to live in countries where order exists and people respect the rules. My response is often, "Brazilians would obey the rules if they were more strictly enforced."

A case in point: in one of my recent trips back to São Paulo, I was driving just over the speed limit at Avenida 23 de Maio, and I noticed that everyone was going "really slow" compared to what I remembered. That's when I noticed speed cameras mounted along the road roughly every 200 yards! Who says that Brazilians cannot follow rules?

Going back to my time in India, the most fascinating aspect of driving there is the hidden code of conduct that is not apparent to the outsider. In Europe, the US and some other first-world countries, street signs exist that signal when to stop, when to go, and who has the right of way. As you learn those rules to pass your driver's license exam, you become more competent as a driver. In India, some of these rules exist, but a more intricate and fascinating unwritten code of conduct is at play. It's not explicit; it's just known.

For instance, when you get to a roundabout, it seems like everyone is entering it at the same time, yet an invisible, magical flow exists that prevents cars from bumping into other cars, tuk-

tuks, motorcycles, bicycles, camels, cows, and/or pedestrians. To a foreigner, drivers in India may seem like they have developed a sixth sense, like those schools of fish swimming in synchrony that we have all seen on nature channels.

In many ways, being a leader in the 21st century is like learning to drive in a different country. Some basic rules exist, like don't run over pedestrians or kill people. But beyond that, the nuances and expectations of leadership do not adhere to a common set of principles and can change depending on what region you find yourself needing to navigate.

Coming from Brazil, I know what it's like not to have rules. Compared to America, Brazil can look like a free-for-all, so where you come from can determine your leadership style, your expectations, and how you communicate.

Leadership in the 21st century needs an internal roadmap. New leaders often feel like they've just climbed behind the wheel of a new car and are on their way to Delhi, only to end up missing the turn at the one-eyed cow and finding themselves in Mumbai. Think of the Samurai Samba Vinci Way™ as the GPS for your new role as a leader. It can get you to your destination and guide you through new territories, helping you gain confidence even if you haven't figured everything out yet. It can help you improve your communication skills and uplevel your executive presence. Because it draws on a centralized set of universal principles on being a great leader, anyone can use this GPS anywhere in the world and experience positive results while avoiding common communication pitfalls and problems, thus increasing trust on the way.

Takeaway Question: In what ways have you changed the way you navigate the new world of work? In what ways could you improve?

Chapter 2: VUCA Rising

When the hi-tech company Uber first arrived on the scene in 2009, it brought the personal transportation industry in some cities to its knees. Representing what has become known as the "sharing economy," Uber's business model is based on an app that allows people to "tap a button, get a ride."

Taxi companies were not excited about Uber. Can you imagine belonging to a sector of the economy that requires you to pay thousands of dollars in "membership" fees only to have a new incumbent playing by a completely different set of rules? That is the reality for cab drivers around the world these days who pay thousands of dollars to have their taxi license and "taxi point" only to see those privileges mean nothing with Uber on the scene.

Naturally, cab drivers stood their ground against Uber's arrival and said, "This is our territory. This is how it's done."

Uber's response? "Not anymore."

As we know, rapid, massive change isn't always received well and can cause emotions to run high. In Brazil, angry cab drivers attacked Uber drivers in retaliation against the disruption Uber was causing to their livelihoods. It reached a point when taxi drivers saw a black car, they'd assume it was an Uber Black;

they would then proceed to break the car's windows, dent the hood and, in a few rare cases, physically hurt the drivers. While violence is never the answer, what the cab drivers did is a perfectly natural emotional response to the threats they felt from change.

This same type of disruption and subsequent retaliation is currently happening in every market around the world in boardrooms, classrooms and cubicles. VUCA is the cause, and it is now the norm rather than the exception in most situations. It has been trending for the past several years, catching many people off guard from first-world countries. Due to these new world conditions, centuries-old institutions including schools, government, and even the church are now being questioned as new and improved models are coming forth. Some are even crumbling to the ground, fast becoming ancient artifacts right before our eyes.

Navigating change has never been easy, but in today's VUCA environment, it can feel almost impossible. VUCA stands for **Volatility, Uncertainty, Complexity and Ambiguity,** and it essentially defines conditions in the 21st century workplace.

When I first heard stories about people who'd never experienced a VUCA environment talking about these conditions, my initial response was, "Oh my God, of course! That's VUCA."

I recognized it right away. I recognized it because VUCA has defined my life since I was two years old. Growing up in a "third world country," I was exposed to volatility, uncertainty, complexity and ambiguity every day. It was my reality.

For those for whom VUCA is new, their response to it is quite different. I can't tell you how many times I've heard clients tell me, "Oh my God, Claudio, we don't know what's happening" as they look around their organization and see nothing but VUCA's handprint on everything.

While having experienced VUCA for as long as I have certainly gives me a slight edge in knowing how to respond in any number of different situations, I am still learning every day how to best address the demands of 21st century leadership.

What does the presence of VUCA mean for organizations and their leaders? For starters, to successfully lead in a VUCA environment requires more than acquiring an external set of skills or focusing on things like wardrobe, posture, and communication style. While these factors have their place, effective leadership also requires addressing who you are being on the inside.

A good analogy to focusing on who you are being on the inside is when you go skydiving. My instructor, Sargento Magalhães, always reminded us that the place to open the reserve parachute is always located in the same region in the body, no matter if we were upside down, twisting, turning, or spinning. The same can be said of navigating in a VUCA environment. No matter what VUCA conditions you have around you, you can always access your internal compass to know what your next move needs to be.

I go into more detail about this in a future chapter, but before I do that, let's look at the problem with most leadership development programs and why so many of them don't take people to their desired destination.

Takeaway Question: How is VUCA present in your company or organization? What is its impact? List three examples.

Chapter 3: The Leadership Development Crisis

Have you ever been required to attend a leadership development workshop sponsored by your company, only to come away wondering why anyone even bothered?

If you answered yes, you are not alone. A 2012 study done by Bersin & Associates found that American companies spend almost US$14 billion annually on leadership development training. Clearly, companies value investing money into educating their talent in solid leadership skills. But are they getting the results they're after? Unfortunately, the answer to this question is "no" more often than not.

The problem isn't the intent. The problem is most leadership development programs don't work that well. Many factors contribute to the high failure rate, including:

- A failure to consider the context of various real-world situations requiring strong leadership skills
- An abysmal retention rate between what is learned in the program and what needs to be done back at work
- Not addressing the deeper level thoughts, feelings, assumptions, and beliefs of workshop participants so the root causes of why they behave the way they do can be addressed and, thus, changed

- Not measuring results

Additionally, many companies are growing so fast these days, they need to promote highly specialized internal candidates into leadership roles to keep them engaged – as they see a career progression and they feel their efforts are being recognized with the promotion. While this approach certainly has its upside, it can also be a disaster if the newly promoted are not properly prepared for the daily demands and responsibilities of their new leadership role. Merely sending them off to a 3-day leadership "bootcamp" isn't going to cut it as effective leadership requires the new leader to embody a new set of behaviors which take time to learn, practice and ultimately internalize.

Given today's highly volatile climate marked by consistent economic fluctuations, re-orgs and subsequent layoffs, 21st century leadership poses a range of challenges. These challenges often arise from three main sources:

- People and situations (external)
- Within the leader him or herself (internal)
- The nature of being a leader in a complex world

As if the VUCA environment wasn't enough, most challenges organizations face tend to show up during times of change or instability, like when a company is being acquired, or a new software system is being introduced to the entire organization. Other triggers that can derail leaders include when a large project or period of work is beginning or ending, or when a group or organization is in transition.

Some challenges are basic and don't last that long (with a clear end date in sight). But many seem to have no end date, like maintaining team morale during another round of layoffs, or keeping everyone focused on the company's long-term mission and vision. These situations can feel a lot like entering a roundabout and getting stuck in a circle with no clear way of getting out.

Real leadership change is possible, but it's not a quick fix. It requires a new model. In the next chapter, I present ideas for what this model can look like.

Takeaway Question: Think about the last professional development seminar you attended. What worked well? What was missing?

Chapter 4: A New Century Calls for a New Model

What also adds to the leadership development crisis is the carryover of outdated leadership models from the 20th century that no longer work in today's business climate.

The rules for effective leadership are different today than they were in the 20th century. Systems, technologies and talent are different today than they were a generation ago. These changes require a new way of looking at how to help subject matter experts (SMEs) show up for and perform at peak levels as leaders in their organizations.

In the 20th century, leadership development was often seen through a top-down model. In the 21st century, leadership development is bottom-up. According to James M. Strock in his book *Serve to Lead*, other differences include:

- Getting the "right" credentials vs. being a lifelong learner
- Looking at things linearly vs. looking at things intuitively
- Focusing on hidden liabilities vs. untapped value
- Autocratic micro-manager vs. coach/conductor
- Giving answers and assertions vs. asking questions

The most common version of leadership training I've seen is sending potential candidates and the newly promoted to a two or three-day leadership development training seminar. Seminars like these are popular, and have nothing inherently wrong with them. The content is usually pretty good, and people do learn things from attending them.

The problem with this approach has to do with behavioral science: Changing fundamental behavior patterns is not possible in a two or three-day workshop and has been proven ineffective in the long run.

Instead, an approach that frequently reinforces the new learned behaviors so that high potentials can grow as leaders has far better results. The best solution involves a combination of training, reading materials, executive coaching and mentoring. That's a cornerstone principle of the SSV Way™; that's the approach I take with my clients.

In a study titled "Executive Coaching as a Transfer of Training Tool: Effects on Productivity in a Public Agency" by Gerald Olivero et. al., researchers concluded that training alone "increased productivity by 22.4 percent." Compared to the training combined with the coaching which included "goal setting, collaborative problem solving, practice, feedback, supervisory involvement, evaluation of end-results, and a public presentation," productivity increased by 88.0 percent, a significantly greater gain compared to training alone.

Because the Samurai Samba Vinci Way™ addresses behavior change rather than putting a Band-Aid on the situation, subject matter experts in new leadership roles have a greater chance at long term success than if they merely attended yet another weekend boot camp.

In the next chapter, I will look specifically at what typically happens to people upon getting promoted to a leadership role.

Takeaway Question: Is the leadership structure in your current organization or company more of a "top-down" or "bottom-up" model?

Chapter 5: So You've Been Promoted. Now What?

I once worked with a man named Pedro, an old-style IT guy in his mid-40s. Pedro always wore a white-shirt with a tie and pens hanging out of a front pocket. He was introverted, more comfortable in front of his computer than in front of his team despite having come a long way since he started working with people.

I began my work with him less than a year after he was promoted to the vice president position of a multibillion-dollar international IT company based in Brazil. Despite his new appointment, Pedro was still spending most of his time coding by hand, even though he was now responsible for over 180 employees under his management.

Pedro came to me because he was great at what he did, but his company kept promoting him to new leadership roles that a) he wasn't trained for and b) took him away from what he loved doing most -- programming. Pedro excelled at tasks that required him to draw on his subject matter expertise rather than leadership skills, and he was struggling.

Even though he felt unprepared for the leadership roles he was promoted to, Pedro accepted them because he loved having his hard work recognized by his department and felt that another opportunity for promotion would not come along if he declined. I have discovered many SMEs face this same kind of pressure to take a promotion even if they don't feel ready. Their fear of missing out overrides any impulse to decline the opportunity.

He eventually reached a point where he couldn't ignore his leadership duties any longer. His team was becoming dysfunctional. Bigger challenges arose such as employee turnover, low morale, and disagreements among team members. These challenges impacted his group's productivity and its ability to deliver their projects on time.

I worked with him to understand:

- Why he was getting paralyzed when it came to dealing with his team
- What skills and competencies were missing (and which ones were strong)
- How to put together a plan of action that worked on areas for improvement that would show some quick results, as well as ensure that his behavior would change in the long run.

The plan included a list of needed skills/competencies along with how he dealt with rejection, difficult conversations, his need for perfectionism and the pervasive inner dialog that goes something like, "I can do it better myself!" We also tackled how to grow, nurture and depend on a strong team by coaching and mentoring a select group of the players.

In my work with him, we focused on some quick wins that would demonstrate that Pedro was working on himself and that people should expect some changes in his department. Some of these changes included making effective requests from his team members, therefore reducing the amount of rework that both he and his team had to do. We also worked on small shifts that helped to change other people's perceptions of him. These were complemented by long-term behavioral changes that we implemented in our year-long engagement.

After working with him, both his and his team's morale increased, employee turnover was dramatically reduced and productivity rose. Becoming more aware of what needed to be changed, coupled with a willingness to implement those changes in his daily life helped Pedro immensely. Having a clear roadmap and a plan of action didn't hurt, either.

Over the years, I have met and worked with many people like Pedro. The fundamental problem is the same: who they are being is not congruent with their new role as a leader.

More times than I can count, I have seen incredibly talented people either passed over for a promotion or floundering in their newly appointed management role because they don't have the skills or competencies necessary to lead. Many of them don't even know what they should know or how others perceive them. This was certainly true for me.

I started my career as a market research coordinator at the Brazilian-arm of an American market research company. My responsibilities included running market research projects, statistical models such as multiple regression analysis, analyzing the data and coordinating fieldwork. I loved the data side of my job as it felt very comfortable. I worked on Lotus 1-2-3 (yeah, I know I am dating myself) and produced presentation decks, as well as full spiral-bound reports.

But I also liked to talk with people and, in my mind, being a good fieldwork coordinator meant being nice to people and delivering great work. I had no idea what to do when someone didn't deliver on my expectations or when I had to have a difficult conversation. That's when I started my quest to discover where I could learn more about leadership as I knew that was a complete blind spot for me.

A common challenge for SMEs is we want to go deeper into our subject matter areas rather than learn new skills like how to lead people. While working as a market research coordinator in Brazil, for example, I was also doing a post-grad course in marketing, followed by another post-grad course in cultural studies. These courses made me want to learn more about semiotics, graphic design and communication in general. That's when I applied to study in Milan, Italy, to complete a specialization in graphic design.

Once I earned my master's degree in interactive multimedia, I was hired as a director of a market research company in the UK which was working with and on the Internet. They were early adopters of data mining and providing online services. Part of my job description was liaising with clients. I didn't know how to do that. I was the typical subject matter expert who knew my area of expertise very well – but nothing about leadership. I was very comfortable with the data, I was very comfortable with the analysis, I was very comfortable generating reports, but I was not comfortable networking or communicating directly with clients, two skills required for effective leadership.

I did not have much of a feel for managing people, yet I was assigned many direct subordinates as well as managing a bigger group of subject matter experts by overseeing the quality of their work. I was completely out of my element, and needed help fast.

As the days wore on in my new role as director, it became more and more clear to me that I did not have the tools to work with people effectively. I did not know how to manage them or how to get the best out of them. I did not know how to deal with clients or client expectations. I had no clue about negotiation skills, influencing skills, leadership skills, or even how to have effective coaching conversations inside the company.

I didn't even know how to talk to my own boss, and he was the owner of the company. Every day I wondered how I could get my ideas across and influence the people I work with? I didn't have an answer, and that put a lot of pressure on me and caused me stress.

One thing was clear: the skills that made me a great subject matter expert were not the skills that would make me great in my promoted position.

During that time, I had a second-degree cousin living in Stuttgart, Germany, so I went to visit him. He was working for Porsche, and I viewed him as a leader. Not only because he was masterful at negotiation, especially multimillion-dollar contracts in different countries, but also because he had executive presence, a concept I explore in a later chapter. I wanted to learn from him and get some tips on how to improve my leadership skills.

We went out for dinner and I asked him, "How do you learn negotiation? I have no clue even where to start."

He said, "Oh, it's easy. You do this, this and that" as he waved his fork through the air as if to emphasize how easy negotiation skills are.

I was shocked. All I could manage to say was, "Uh, okay" as we continued with our meal. We had a very nice conversation, but I didn't learn anything related to what I had come there for in the first place.

Ultimately, being promoted forced me to look at my own life and say, "Okay, I have these core competencies that I can draw on to be better at what I'm doing now. But there are a lot of gaps I need to fill." Recognizing that those gaps existed for me propelled me into action. Over the next few years, I invested heavily into my self-education. I read books. I enrolled in courses. I attended seminars on subjects I knew would help advance my career. But even after all that time and money I invested, I still didn't know everything to be an effective leader. If only I had the SSV Way™!

Knowing what I know now about the power of the SSV Way™, I would be quick to tell the Claudio I was back then (a newly appointed Claudio), "Claudio, develop this SSV model as fast as you can and follow what it says. We don't have time to waste!" I would soon discover that sometimes the best breakthroughs come from experiencing the hardest times.

Takeaway Question: In what ways do you relate to Pedro's story? How does my personal story of promotion into a leadership role ring true for you or people you work with?

Chapter 6: With Your Promotion Comes an Amazing Opportunity

As a newly promoted employee, I had to learn how to be a leader through a combination of book study and putting into practice what I was learning on the front line. It wasn't easy. It took time. But it was worth it.

While it's true we can get better by doing what we learn through study, I also don't believe just doing is enough. The best combination with the highest probability of internalizing new skills involves learning and doing simultaneously. If we learn just by doing, we're probably going to have holes in our learning. If we just learn theory without implementing the concepts, we're not going to know how to apply them when faced with real world situations.

Learning on paper does not prepare us for life's curve balls. The last time I checked, life throws a lot of curveballs, especially in negotiating and influencing scenarios. What happens in real life is almost never like what is presented on paper.

On paper, everything is beautiful. Everything is clean. Everything always works out during role playing exercises. But when the real deal comes along, rarely does the situation follow the exact script presented in the text book. We are on our own, working with what we have in the moment.

As a newly promoted leader, you are more than likely having to learn as you go without a lot of time for book study. While you may be feeling a bit out of sorts, please recognize that you have an incredible opportunity. Your promotion is exciting for a lot of reasons. You have a new title. You're advancing up the career ladder you've worked so hard to climb. You're going to be earning more money and perhaps some bonuses or some perks that you weren't privy to before.

You also have an opportunity to emerge from your cocoon of subject matter greatness to really start making a difference to your organization and the people on your team who see you as someone to look up to and respect in your new role.

Isn't that an incredible gift? To be in a position of influence leading others so your organization's initiatives get off the ground, run smoothly and result in exciting outcomes the company celebrates?

It is, but...

As I quickly discovered, being a manager/vice president/ director is very different from being a subject matter expert. Most people who get promoted to a managerial position are not prepared for the demands and responsibilities of their new position.

Over the years, I've worked with countless people who have been in this exact position who -- while very excited about their new role -- don't have any idea how to do it well. They get started with a lot of enthusiasm only to discover things aren't going very well. Difficult employees, new demands on their time, and not being able to rely on existing SME skills to get them through are but a few of the challenges they face.

Is it any surprise most people retreat into what's comfortable and familiar? They frequently ask me, "Claudio, why is it so difficult to make the transition from my area of expertise to being a really good leader?"

I wish I had an easy answer. Becoming a great leader requires a commitment, the willingness to put in the work and the self-discipline necessary to master these new skills. It requires a willingness to ask yourself tough questions and be brutally honest with your answers. It means opening yourself to the input of a trusted coach or mentor who can hold you accountable as you work on your transformation. And it involves having an open mind -- what is often referred to as being "coachable and teachable" -- as you begin your new journey toward leadership.

I visited my cousin in Germany with the hopes of gaining new insights about how to lead better. What that experience taught me is how difficult explaining leadership skills can be for those who already have them.

Yet if established leaders can't show new and emerging leaders how to lead, who can?

In the next few chapters, I will share with you some best practices for making the transition from subject matter expert to leader as smooth as possible.

Takeaway Question: Who do you turn to when you have questions about how to lead more effectively?

Chapter 7: Back to the Beginning

I remember when I was in dire financial difficulty, over US $100,000 in debt. I had to drop everything that I was doing and focus solely on climbing out of the enormous hole I'd dug for myself.

Before that, I was participating in a lot of deliberate mindfulness work. It was not called "mindfulness" at the time, but I was doing a lot of it. I was investing in personal growth experiences, as well. Once I realized how bad my financial situation had become, I dropped everything to focus solely on surviving. My daily mantra became, "Okay, so how can I pay next month's rent?"

As that old saying goes from airline safety, you need to put on your oxygen mask first before helping others or else you're going to pass out. You cannot help anyone if you aren't first taking care of yourself. I learned this lesson the hard way, and I will never forget it.

Once you move out of survival mode, then helping others naturally follows. If you are still struggling, let's say financially or with your health, of course you're going to be thinking about yourself and no one else. Of course, you're going to be thinking about, how can I survive? It's very difficult to see the bigger picture when you're trying to survive. If we think about Maslow's Hierarchy of Needs, our basic needs like food, shelter, and safety have to be fulfilled first before we can consider reaching our full potential.

In terms of the Samurai Samba Vinci Way™, when you're a subject matter expert and you get promoted, you're leaving the top of a triangle of expertise and starting out at the bottom of a new one called leadership. Suddenly, everything is brand new. You don't have a clear sense of how to show up according to your new role. You haven't worked through the stages yet; it's not uncommon to feel any combination of lost, incompetent and helpless. Not exactly what you signed up for!

To go from being seen as the go-to person -- the subject matter expert, the person who has all the degrees and maybe has written tons of papers or contributed to all kinds of talk shows -- to being the new kid, with a brand-new title and a host of responsibilities, is not easy. Frankly, it's really hard being a beginner again! In many ways, we may feel like we are in deep debt, with no clear way of getting out. But unless we are willing to go through that initial awkward stage of becoming a leader, we can't grow. We'll always be stuck in the past.

Will you know how to do everything effectively from day one? Of course not. There will be days when you're going to feel like you are constantly reaching for that proverbial oxygen mask. That's okay. This transition is huge and you don't want to take it lightly.

So let's be selfish for a little while and recalibrate the being part of you as a first step.

Bob Dunham from the Institute for Generative Leadership has a beautiful concept for this situation. Specifically, he talks about the importance of being a beginner. You need to not only know what it feels like, but also to accept being a beginner again. Acceptance is key because you are going from being the top expert in your field -- the one with all the answers -- to suddenly being someone who doesn't know the first thing about leading a team. The two roles rely on completely different competencies.

Just because you're a beginner doesn't mean you can't have strength, however. Ram Charan talks about this concept in his notebooks, referring to different inflection points of high-potential leaders. When you're getting promoted, how do you need to be spending your time? What percentage of your time is doing and what percentage of your time is mentoring people? What percentage of time is communicating with others? What work values do you need to identify and prioritize?

For some newly-minted leaders who are required to mentor others, mentoring people can feel like a waste of time because it draws on soft skills as opposed to hands-on work. What managers are producing can't be seen, and that can be difficult for people who are used to generating tangible results like software programs or widgets. They don't see how working with a team can be more productive than trying to accomplish tasks alone. Yet successfully managing that team is a crucial component to achieving big goals.

Bob also talks about the value of teams. A team exists because you cannot handle everything all by yourself. A team exists because you're making a much bigger promise to your organization than what you can offer by yourself. That's why a team exists. Rather than seeing your team as an obstacle to solving problems you have tackled on your own in the past, see it instead as a vehicle for making new discoveries and successfully tackling even bigger challenges.

Instead of seeing this transition as a burden, instead of seeing this as something to be gotten past quickly, see it as a chance to become something more: a bigger and better version of yourself. Be open to being a beginner again and investing the time it takes to learn the rules of the leadership road. The journey is pretty cool, and certainly worth your time. Before you know it, you will have developed the new skills necessary to lead effectively and look back fondly at this time when you were just starting out.

Takeaway Question: When have you felt like a beginner? How did you deal with it?

Chapter 8: 21ˢᵗ Century Leadership Is about Who You Are Being

A few years ago, I was hired by a high-powered global IT company in New York City to run a three-day workshop at the new World Trade Center. They brought me in to work with their legal team. In the weeks leading up to this event, I remember talking to someone who had been teaching leadership courses for 30 years.

I described the nature of the workshop to her, mentioning I'd be working with lawyers who had been negotiating multi-million dollar contracts for more than two decades. I explained I would be delivering material on advanced negotiation skills, among other things.

When I told her that I was going to focus more on who they were being and less on leadership frameworks and techniques (because they'd already learned about plenty of those), she said, "Good luck with that, Claudio" in a tone that implied, "Yeah, you're going to flop."

At that time, I had not yet developed the Samurai Samba Vinci Way™ into what it is today. My time with them marked the start of its development and they loved it. They loved it because we were talking about the things that nobody talks about in typical leadership development programs, namely how to actually be a leader.

More times than not, we place too much emphasis on the external characteristics of leadership and not enough on the internal. Think about your own perception of a leader. What immediately comes to mind? Traditionally, leadership in first-world countries is about external cues like appearance, skin color, and gender. Not much time or effort is invested in what lies beneath the surface, like intuition, mindset, beliefs and emotions.

One of the central themes of the SSV Way™ is the importance of taking time to focus on developing a core set of values -- essentially, a way of being – so we can be armed with the tools to succeed in any situation anywhere in the world. Indeed, being a leader is more than just a title, or the clothes we wear, or the contracts we close. Being a leader, at its core, is about who we are on the inside and how we show up each day to work with the people in our charge.

When people first begin working with me, they often tell me, "Claudio, I'm not very intuitive."

My response is always the same. I say, "Yes, you may not be an intuitive person right now; that's because you have not been exercising this muscle. If I told you to pick up 100 pounds off the floor, would you be able to do so? Maybe not right now. If you train hard enough through deliberate practice, you would develop the strength to pick up 100 pounds off the floor. A similar approach will garner you a stronger intuition."

Working to overcome common personal traits that can prevent us from doing our job well needs to be a top priority for anyone who wants to build trust and lead teams in a VUCA marketplace. I will go into more detail about these common personal traits in a later chapter, but for now I will tell you they include working through insecurity, defensiveness, an inability to be objective, indecision, and impatience. These traits are arguably the most common roadblocks new leaders face as they embark on their journey. These traits have no place at the table of 21st leadership, and often hinder progress and cause all kinds of havoc within organizations.

Takeaway Question: What external factors of leadership have you valued in the past? What specific character traits do you believe are important in an effective leader?

Chapter 9: Shaving Seconds off the Leadership Game

I used to play tennis quite a lot. When I was playing, Martina Navratilova was the one to beat. Today, the one to beat is Serena Williams.

In tennis, playing at the regional level is one thing; playing at the nationals is another. And playing on the bigger stages like the French Open or Wimbledon is a completely different game. The same can be said for the Olympics. You can be the best tennis player in the country, but when you arrive to compete at the international level, every millisecond of your serve, your anticipation and your return counts.

One second can make the entire difference between coming in first or fourth place. Success literally boils down to shaving seconds off our game. My tennis coach Toninho used to spend time helping me develop better awareness of not just my techniques, but also on who I was being as a tennis player. He helped me improve my backhand, and he also helped me improve my state of mind. He was fond of reminding me not to worry so much about being perfect, but instead to focus on what I needed to accomplish to win.

Unfortunately, I was my own worst enemy with respect to

getting better. For starters, I spent way too much time focusing on the angle of the racquet and where the ball was going on the court rather than listening to what Toninho was telling me. Those details about racquet angle and ball positioning mattered very little in the grand scheme of things.

I also had a terrible habit of being hard on myself when I made a mistake. The Samurai in me wouldn't settle for anything less than perfection. Wanting to be perfect was getting in the way of me winning. So was being reactive when my opponents did things that irked me. I remember one opponent named Fabio who loved to make me run from one side of the court to the other, even during practice. My thought was, "Come on! We are just practicing here. Stop making me run like a crazy chicken!" What I failed to recognize was Fabio wasn't making me do anything. I was choosing to react rather than step back and see I had other choices.

Finally, my desire to be nice to everyone got in the way of me winning more games. I remember playing in a tournament at my tennis club. I was 17 years old and I went up against a man in his mid-forties who wasn't very good. Because I felt badly for him, I let him win. Losing would make me feel badly about myself, and the vicious cycle of beating myself up over bad decisions would start all over again.

Winning at anything often comes down to breaking out of the negative habit loops we create for ourselves the way I did when I was playing tennis. We see it in sports; it happens in leadership, too. The intangibles like mindset and thinking for possibility play a far bigger role in our ability to succeed than we may at first give them credit for. Because we can't see these things, we don't always know what we need to work on. This can be especially true for someone who transitions from being an expert in an area that's data-driven into a leadership role where most of what is expected from us is abstract and unquantifiable.

The intangibility of our new leadership role may cause us to think, "I don't even know where to start. I don't even know what the metrics are." When my team and I are working with someone on becoming a world-class leader, we focus most of our time on strengthening what's not obvious.

As a coach, I have helped engineers, research scientists, Nobel laureates, astro-physicists, IT experts and other specialists who rise to leadership positions favorably improve their game and navigate the unfamiliar waters of their new role through a process that helps them understand who they are being as a leader.

As I've established, many SMEs like the ones listed above are promoted into management positions because of their technical knowledge and skill. They often possess fantastic technique. They aren't bad people -- in fact, they are often eager to perform well in their new role. What they often lack is exposure to solid leadership training on how to actually be leaders. When faced with the new responsibilities and challenges of leading teams, they resort to what's familiar to them as subject matter experts (SMEs), falling back into their comfort zones.

While returning to their comfort zones gives these experts a sense of control over uncertain or chaotic situations, the long-range consequences of not being properly trained can be disastrous -- for them and their organizations.

Leadership books abound. A quick search on Amazon using the keyword leadership generates close to 200,000 matches. On Google, 187 million matches! When we think about leadership development, well-known names like John Maxwell always make the top of the list. He's probably the biggest name from the US.

While some of these resources are useful, what's powerful about the Samurai Samba Vinci Way™ compared to other leadership development books is how I focus more on who we are being and less on a set of skills. Other leadership guides emphasize frameworks, with suggestions such as, "Here is how you deal with situation X or situation Y." These approaches have some merit, but they ultimately fail to address who we are being when we're solving problems.

This is one of the biggest reasons I was so successful with the lawyers. We didn't just focus on the techniques of leadership. We invested time into changing on the inside, going deep. I have found that when we apply a technique without changing who we are, then we can be as ineffective as we were when we didn't have the technique in the first place.

Or worse. Because more times than not, simply applying a technique leads to more problems, leaving us wondering, "What is happening here?" Putting another Band-Aid technique on the gaping wound isn't going to do much, and is often pointless.

To avoid gaping wounds in our leadership experiences, we need to ask a central question: "How do I become better at being me so I can work with people and not alienate them, upset them, while inspiring them to do what I need them to do for the company?" One way to do this is by working with a coach. Had I not had Toninho pointing out my blind spots, I never would have gained the awareness needed to change and improve my game.

Investing time into answering this question will get us far better results with our teams in the long run than reaching for the first-aid kit every time someone comes to us bleeding.

It's very simple: either we're getting prepared to play at our new level or we're not.

Takeaway Questions: How are you being as a person, as a company and as a culture right now? Who do you need to be so you can play at a new level? What do you need to do to get to play at that level?

Chapter 10: Working in the Space of Not Knowing

A key experience that has helped me shape the SSV Way™ is living in several countries over a short span of time and becoming familiar with what I call the "space of not knowing." Brazil, Japan, Italy, and then to England, the UK was my fourth country in as many years. In many ways, being promoted is like traveling to a foreign country for the first time. Moving around as much as I did, I was constantly forced to adapt to different cultures. I had to continuously ask myself, *who am I?*

During those formative years, I wasn't clear about my core values. It was, therefore, all too easy to adopt as my own the dominant persona of the country in which I was living rather than show up fully myself from a place of strength and confidence. When I was in Japan, for example, I behaved much more like the Samurai: quiet and rigid. When I was in Brazil, I was more playful, with a "go with the flow" attitude. In Italy, I spent most of my time thinking of new ideas, being creative, and living a Bohemian lifestyle, core elements of a Vinci.

Italy is much more like Brazil in terms of being very outgoing, but there were other elements at play, too, because I was living in Milan. Milan is the capital of fashion and also, it is a place where high precision manufacturing takes place. This is where

Milan's strong Samurai ethos of mastery grows alongside its Vinci roots. The Samba was alive and well after dark; a friend of mine was dating a catwalk model, and she arranged for us to get into different discos and hip parties. I had a lot of fun as I spent a good percentage of my time in the Quadrilatero, which is the most expensive part of Milan, with Gucci, Bulgari and other designer stores on every corner. For the first time, I was beginning to see how the three personas could coexist and create possibilities for me.

But complete clarity about the SSV Way™ was still a few years away. After Italy, I arrived in the UK and discovered it moved at a completely different pace than anywhere I'd been before. Especially in London, a multicultural city, I got completely lost. I hadn't developed my core strengths or values, and I didn't yet know how to stand in my strength. As a result, I was like a paper bag floating in the wind of everyone else's agenda.

Another factor influencing my lost state of mind was not knowing anyone in London. As soon as I arrived, I was knocking on doors. I had just enough money to make it for three months. I established myself in a bed and breakfast there, and then I bought a prepaid cell phone just to have a number so that companies I applied to could contact me.

The company I had been working with in Brazil had written an introduction letter to a British company they had a partnership with. They introduced me to the CEO of that bigger company, which was the AC Nielsen of the UK. It's called MORI.

So in February, I met with MORI's president and CEO.

He said, "Claudio, we're not really looking for anyone right now. Actually, I don't think that this Internet thing is going to go anywhere anyway, especially for market research."

It was the mid-90s and the Internet was in its infancy. Regardless, I was frankly shocked that he didn't see the potential I saw in the Internet. Are you kidding me? I thought. This information super highway is a branding opportunity unlike any other I'd ever seen!

But he was adamant. "There are these guys that we work with. They do technology. I'll connect you with them."

While it didn't sound like the perfect fit, I still said, "Okay. Let's have a conversation."

I showed up for the interview and was told they weren't anticipating having any openings until September. Now remember, this was February. I had money to last me through the end of April, early May at the latest. I didn't have five extra months to wait around for something to open.

Through a chain of referrals, I finally landed at a global PR company that specializes in reputation management. I was connected to a man named Stephen and when he discovered what I brought to the table, he said, "Claudio, you need to work with us because what you do and your vision for this is brilliant."

That was my first hiring in the UK, and at that time I was just another subject matter expert. I eventually took a year off to complete my Masters in Interactive Multimedia because I really wanted to go much deeper in that area of expertise.

Then, when I left, that's when I got a managerial position at another market research company that specialized in using the Internet. I still remember hearing them say things like, "Can you imagine when we're going to be talking to our phones by looking at it instead of putting it on the side?" We weren't talking about those types of phone features in early 2000s. It was much earlier than even SMS and other smartphone-based communication platforms. This was around the time when I got promoted to the managerial and then director level.

Moving had its upside. I gained tremendous insights about core values and which ones I wanted to make my own. It forced me to ask hard questions of myself and do the work I needed to become better.

Many of us are raised in a society where not knowing the answer is unacceptable. We learn in school that we need to have the answer but not ask the question. In fact, having the answers and not asking the questions gets rewarded. Why is this? Why is being in the space of not knowing something to be avoided, punished and feared?

One of the hallmarks of a Samurai Samba Vinci leader is her willingness to embrace the space of not knowing. It sets her apart from leaders who feel they need to know all the answers before they can possibly lead.

If you come from the space of not knowing, you're really going to learn. Having lived in five countries, I've had to constantly question why things are done a certain way. The most common answer I've heard is along the line of "because that's the way it's done." Right away, that answer puts up a barrier to both parties in the conversation. The person saying that has closed off the channel of possibility for doing it a way that may not be familiar; the person hearing that may immediately shut down because they don't feel heard or worse, feel dismissed.

I remember working with a financial institution as a consultant and they wanted to implement some new banking transaction systems like electronic deposits and bank transfers. I told them about the telephone banking system we had in Brazil. It was very advanced out of necessity and I saw an opportunity for this institution to model their new system after it. Without missing beat, they implied that they had nothing to learn from a third world country. At the time, I was still operating in the space of not knowing how to stand in my strength as an SSV leader, so I simply shrugged my shoulders and said, "Okay."

Everyone lost that day. I lost the opportunity to stand up for something I knew would work; they lost the opportunity to add millions of pounds to their profit margins and be seen as an industry leader.

Today, I personally love going through the space of not knowing. It offers a chance to revisit how we do things and how we can improve; it allows for creativity to flourish; and ultimately, it's a great place to grow!

Takeaway Questions: Think about a time when you didn't know the answer. How did it make you feel? What did you do to solve the problem?

Chapter 11: Being the Best for the World vs. in the World

One of the goals of becoming a Samurai Samba Vinci leader is to move from being the best in the world to being the best for the world. What, exactly, is the difference?

Being the best in the world involves reaching the highest pinnacle of expertise in any given area. Think of Steve Jobs, Oprah Winfrey, and Lady Diana as examples of famous individuals who have achieved the highest pinnacle of their respective specializations. Steve Jobs mastered the design of the iPhone, a device that has revolutionized the way we communicate around the world. Oprah Winfrey is known as the Queen of daytime talk TV and has built an empire around the concept of living our best lives. Lady Diana was an ambassador for her country and symbolic of what we can all aspire to be.

We can take each one of these people to the next step, however, namely to being the best for the world, too.

Why?

Because they are no longer working to achieve something for themselves. They focus their attention on serving others.

There is a massive difference between those who are playing at the top and those who are still working their way to the top.

For instance, when I'm working with a Nobel Prize winner as opposed to a manager at a Fortune 500 company, I witness two very different behaviors.

Generally speaking, a manager is still trying to prove himself by becoming the best in the world while a Nobel Prize winner is simply being himself with nothing more to prove. He has room to have fun because he knows that he is the best in the world at what he does. He is now focusing his attention on being the best for the world. He does a lot of work with charities. He does a lot of work with his own foundation for education and scholarships. He invests time in mentoring others and raising up leaders. He's done the internal work, so he can do great external work.

The actor Matt Damon is another example of someone who is the best in the world. For many years, he has worked hard on becoming the best at his craft, honing his skills, working with professional coaches and mentors who help him get better. Known for his award-winning performances in movies like *Good Will Hunting* and *The Martian*, he now uses his fame and fortune to help out with humanity-based causes that go beyond his own work as a means of being the best for the world.

To make this shift successfully, we need to acknowledge the barriers that stand in our way so we can effectively move past them. Common barriers to being the best for the world include specific personal traits I mentioned in chapter 8. Too often the following characteristics block us from fully actualizing our leadership capabilities:

- Insecurity
- Defensiveness

- An inability to be objective
- Indecision
- Impatience

Take a moment to reflect on the most recent time you can recall operating under the influence of one or more of these traits. Just like too much alcohol can impair our judgment, cognitive processing and motor skills, so too can these emotional toxins interfere with leading effectively and ultimately achieving the results we want.

I like to tell the story about the first time I presented something in front of a group of about 15 to 18 people to illustrate how these negative personal traits can get in the way of reaching our goals. As I pushed my chair away from the protection of the table to stand up, my hands were shaking so much that the piece of paper I was holding transformed into a means of fanning myself. My voice would not come out, and my throat was as dry as the Arizona desert. I couldn't even remember what I had to say because I completely blacked out. And all they had asked me to do was introduce myself and talk about what I did! My insecurity levels were off the chart. Looking back, I'm amazed I made it through the day.

These days, when people see me presenting anything or communicating with anyone, they say, "Oh my God, Claudio, you're a natural." I always chuckle because I am anything but "a natural." I worked hard on overcoming my insecurities to get better at making presentations. I can confidently say I am very good at doing that now, and my next goal is to become better at presenting on camera. Because so much of my client work takes place using video conferencing, my next level is being able to look into a camera and feel comfortable.

For many of us, wanting to become the best in the world at what we do is perfectly natural. We invest years of our lives to get the education, the training and the hands-on experiences to achieve expert status and all the rewards that come with our achievement. When we consciously decide we want to move to that next level of being the best for the world, we must be willing to face our limitations head on, even if it feels awkward or uncomfortable. Strengthening our self-awareness is one way to move past the barriers that keep us hemmed in to old patterns of behavior and thought.

In the next section, I will share with you the gifts of each persona and how you can use those gifts to become not just the best in the world, but the best for the world, too as you lead yourself, your team and your organization toward 21st century success.

Takeaway Questions: Which of the five barriers listed in this chapter give you the most trouble? Can you recall a story when you were able to push past your barriers? What would becoming the best for the world mean to you?

PART II:
THE THREE GIFTS

Chapter 12: Your Samurai Samba Vinci Profile

Now that you understand the context and value of the SSV Way™ for guiding you on your leadership journey, let's determine which of the three personas you are most like.

So, are you a Samurai, Samba or Vinci? To discover your primary profile, take a few minutes right now to complete the SSV Profile Assessment online. I have also included a downloadable version of the self-assessment for those readers who like old fashioned paper and pencil. Once you have your score, you can return to the book to dive deeper into each profile.

Visit **www.toyamaco.com/ssvbook** to access the SSV Profile Assessment.

Key questions to ask yourself when thinking about your primary persona include:
- What characteristics best describe me?
- How would others describe me?
- How do I connect to the other two profiles?
- Why am I more like one of these profiles than another?

Asking these questions is often where I begin when working with clients. Their answers give me clues about their dominant persona, which allows me to tailor their training experience accordingly. Please keep in mind that no one persona is better than the other two. In fact, each profile has unique gifts that enhance our workplace cultures as well as our communities, schools, and private homes. I will share the gifts of each persona in the coming chapters.

Here are some highlights of the Samurai, Samba and Vinci profiles:

Samurai

Samurais know their core and who they truly are. They tend not to show emotion and are often described as deep thinkers. They don't get easily pushed around emotionally. They are centered. With a strong core, empathy is possible without getting dragged into people's dramas. Samurais tend to be on an even emotional keel, not becoming overly excited or down.

Samba

Sambas score high on emotional intelligence spectrums. They love talking to people and tend to be excellent communicators. Sambas also tend to be great people connectors and bring some joie de vivre to work. They adapt easily to change and learn quickly how others communicate. They are flexible and operate with a spirit of fun.

Vinci

Vincis appreciate ideas and beauty above just about everything else. They are creative and need to take time to take pleasure in the finer things in life. They don't like to be rushed, and they hate being boxed in. As my friend Anna says, "Just get rid of the box. Box, be gone!" Vincis go beyond the notion of "thinking outside of the box." Vincis want to eliminate the box altogether.

In some cases, people who take the SSV assessment discover they score close or equally to two personas. When we combine two personas together, we get some interesting mixes. For instance, a Samurai without Samba means no spark. Like the old proverb that warns, all work and no play makes Jack a dull boy, operating as a Samurai all the time without taking a break from work can make a person become both bored and boring. Likewise, the Samba without the Samurai means no structure at worst, a loose structure at best. Too much play and not enough work can lead to challenges of a different sort. Finally, a Samurai without any Vinci means very little innovation; no Samurai with Vinci means possibly never settling on one idea to pursue.

This is but one example of how mixing elements from the three personas can elevate our leadership capabilities and help us become highly effective in our leadership role. When we understand our core persona, communicating with others also becomes less complicated and more effortless.

Change begins with awareness, and I had to develop keener awareness around my communication style once I began leading teams. When I was first working in the UK, my communication style was very blunt, in Samurai fashion. When I interacted with people, I could see in some of their eyes how much they did not like my direct approach; some of them physically recoiled from me. British culture likes to use decorative language and a lot of words to express ideas. They do not like a "Boom, here it is" style at all.

Almost immediately, I could see that I was scaring some people with my direct communication style. I soon realized I needed to adapt how I said things while operating in the British culture with its emphasis on embellished sentences and longer explanations for concepts. This discovery helped me tremendously as I could meet people on their terms instead of imposing my style on them.

Another way of thinking about the differences among the three personas can be explained through a description of what it's like to ride a train in Tokyo, São Paulo, and Prague, respectively.

I will start with what it's like to take the train in Tokyo. When I was living there, my train was scheduled to arrive at 7:03 a.m., and at 7:03 a.m., the train arrived. Never late, never early. Always precisely on time at exactly 7:03. People wearing white gloves pushed all us passengers into the train compartments, and everything was coordinated down to the last detail.

At first, I had a difficult time adjusting to this ultra-efficient way of riding the train, but I quickly realized that if I was going to succeed in Japanese society, I needed to become more regimented. I needed to become more subdued. I needed to adjust to their culture and become more like the Samurai.

Taking the train in São Paulo is a very different experience from the one in Tokyo. First of all, Brazil doesn't have many trains because they have followed in America's footsteps with its car-centered culture. In the last few years, however, trains have made a resurgence, but there aren't nearly the number of trains Japan has. And when Brazil's trains do run, they are Samba all the way -- improvised, and going with the flow.

Prague offers the best example of a Vinci train-riding experience. The moment you step into one of Prague's metro stations, it's instantly clear that the engineers behind designing them were Vincis. The stations are clean and beautiful. Futuristic architecture can be seen everywhere. An air of possibility and a nod to future generations prevails. It's no surprise that some of Prague's train stations are considered the finest in Europe.

The Samurai Samba Vinci leadership train is pulling into the station of companies and organizations around the world. With your new insights about your primary persona, you hold a ticket to board it and ride it to your next destination. Once you understand why you are the way you are, changing becomes easier; so does saying good bye to who you used to be.

In the next three chapters, I'll explore each persona in more detail, starting with the Samurai.

Chapter 13: The Gift of the Samurai

The gift of the Samurai has its roots in Japanese culture that includes the country's long history of sword making, hosting ceremonial tea parties, and rolling sushi. Each of these traditions contribute to the ethos of the Samurai persona, which includes determination, discipline, and aiming for perfection.

There's a precision and a beauty inherent to each tradition. Like the sword maker or the tea master, people who are fundamentally Samurai perfect their techniques as they excel at their chosen area of expertise.

Key characteristics of the Samurai include:
- Awareness of what is needed to show the world your authentic self (this is where the shift from what people expect from you to being true to your core comes in)
- Understanding the difference between repetition and recurrence
- Respect for perfecting the process
- Competence
- Integrity
- Honor

A Samurai is not interested in instant gratification, multitasking, and staying on top of popular culture. A Samurai is often deeply focused on one thing at a time and does not get distracted by frivolous matters. Whereas a black belt in karate in western society is the ultimate goal for participants, achieving black belt in Japanese society is only the beginning of a lifelong commitment. Correctly practicing the basic moves again and again so when the time to fight comes around, the Samurai is completely prepared to meet his opponent.

Mr. Miagi in the popular film *The Karate Kid* symbolizes the ways of the Samurai. His mantra of "wax on, wax off" could be a Samurai's mantra, as well. In Japan, years -- if not decades -- are needed to learn something. In the west, however, the prevailing attitude is often, how can I do this task in five minutes or less?

Bob Dunham of the Institute for Generative Leadership talks about the difference between repetition and recurrence. Repetition is performing the same move over and over. It doesn't require paying full attention; you can be repeating the movement while thinking of something else.

Recurrence, on the other hand, demands being fully present to what you are doing. It is a mindful practice where deep awareness plays a key role. Mastering a technique through repetition, and then mastering a discipline through recurrence is how respect is gained. The Samurai persona commands this level of respect.

Integrity is very important to the Samurai persona. Historically, making a mistake brings tremendous dishonor to a Samurai's family; a true Samurai would prefer death to dishonor. While this may seem extreme to those who are not primarily Samurai, it is very real to those who are. The honor, the determination, and the ethos of doing the right thing are fundamental to a Samurai's nature.

Mindfulness is also at play these days. The practice of stilling the mind and asking yourself, "So what am I standing for? What is really happening here?" can assist leaders in making good decisions.

People who are predominantly Samurai make for great:

- Engineers
- Scientists
- Mathematicians
- Project Managers
- CFOs
- COOs

When I'm teaching about the three personas, I like to use my hands to demonstrate the essence of each persona. For the Samurai leader, here's what it looks likes. Put both hands together, palm to palm with your fingers pointing toward the sky. Place the tips of the fingers of your right hand at the base of the palm of your left hand. Now align your two hands in that position between your eyes, with the fingertips of your left hand lining up with the spot between your eyebrows.

The Samurai trusts his natural reflexes and decisions because of his extensive training and practice. He is calm and strong, with narrowed, focused eyes set clearly on his goal. This does not mean that the Samurai doesn't see what's in his peripheral vision; instead, his steady gaze reinforces his focus. The Samurai walks deliberately as well, leading each step with his heel first as if in a slow-motion scene in an action film. Fire, explosions and fighting could be happening simultaneously, but the Samurai leader calmly takes out the villain who is brave enough to try to attack him from the side. He breathes deeply from his diaphragm; his breaths are long, full and slow. His posture is perfectly erect and he trusts his skeleton and muscles to carry his weight the way they were designed to do. This is the Samurai leader's power pose. You can feel the core strength flowing through your body when you conduct this pose. To see a video demonstrating the Samurai power pose, visit **www.toyamaco. com/ssvbook**

Now let's look at the gift of the Samba.

Chapter 14: The Gift of the Samba

As we saw in the previous chapter, the Samurai persona has an air of seriousness to it. In this chapter, I will show you how Samba is the opposite of the Samurai, with an emphasis on color, fun, and play. To understand the essence of the Samba better, allow me to share a story about Brazil's Carnival.

It was a hot summer afternoon as I stood on the beach in São Paulo State, surrounded by hundreds of people. We all moved in a wave of humanity, caught up in the rhythm of the drums. That steady beat hummed through my body and reminded me of how amazing it is to be alive, to be a part of something as magical as Carnival.

The word Samba is a Brazilian musical genre and dance style, with African roots particularly of Angola and the Congo, as well as the samba de roda genre of the northeastern Brazilian state of Bahia. When you are in a Samba's presence, it's easy to get swept up in their energy and joie de vivre, just like it's easy to get swept up in the flow on the streets at Carnival. It's colorful, it's beautiful and then of course, you have the drums.

One of the things I like most about Carnival is the sound of the drums piercing through my body, making every molecule shake with the rhythm. When you are close to the "bateria" (drums), there is no way of avoiding being swept away by this rich rhythm. It literally makes your whole body vibrate, and the confluence of the different sound instruments is simply magical.

Like Brazilians, the instruments used in Carnival have different origins, starting with the afoxé, which is a traditional Brazilian instrument with African origins. The afoxé consists of a gourd (cabaça) wrapped in a net in which beads are threaded. Next is the Atabaque, a percussion instrument made of Jacaranda wood, with the top covered with leather. The Pandeiro - another musical instrument that came to Brazil from Portugal, derived from an earlier Arabic or Moorish instrument still found in North Africa -- has a tunable drumhead and metal jingles ("platinelas" in Portuguese) on the sides. These are just three of the dozen instruments used in the Carnival that contribute to the rich blend of sounds.

The rhythmic cadence is hypnotizing, and can put you in a trance-like state. Carnival happens in February which is still summer in Brazil. Summers in Brazil are hot, with beautiful blue skies decorated with sparse clouds. Happiness is contagious and palpable; it's impossible for attendees not to start moving our bodies to the rhythm with a smile on our faces. Everyone jumps up and down, hands in the air and clapping as we sing in sync with the music. Even the singer and musicians are enjoying themselves, dancing to the rhythm as they play.

Formal introductions are unnecessary to start talking with people around us. I love the informality of human connection that these moments present. Everything flows beautifully. The colorfulness of the surroundings combined with everyone wearing bright oranges, reds, yellows, greens, and blues adds to the happy atmosphere. Extremely cold beer, what we Brazilians call "cerveja de canto de freezer" (translated as beer that was stored in the corner of a freezer), is readily available and adds to the overall experience.

This scene describes the beauty of Carnival and captures the essence of the Samba way. Happiness, connection and a celebration of life are three of the fundamental aspects of a Samba persona.

I witnessed this energy when I worked with the global marketing director of an IT company with close to $4B US annual revenue who needed to work on her executive presence so that she could command more respect from her team and her peers. She had to step up big time in terms of not only her posture but also her gravitas, being a big player in the world arena as it's known.

A Samba through and through, Lily continued to demonstrate the mentality and work behaviors that were congruent with her previous job title even after she had been promoted. She had yet to align who she was being with her new leadership role. In her new role, she had a tremendous responsibility of representing the company worldwide, working at a demanding pace with high levels of exposure that very few people get to experience.

In the beginning of our time together, we worked on what was missing in terms of her own perception of herself. We started with interviewing her bosses to understand what their views of and expectations for her were. We also interviewed her to understand what she expected from the new role and what her perception was in terms of her strengths and weaknesses when tackling this new role.

Based on the data we collected from these interviews, we understood that we needed to work on helping her be less hands-on and more of a mentor to other team members. At the same time, we needed to help her increase her profile at the global executive position that she was asked to step into. We also identified that she liked to collaborate with others, but she wasn't very keen on managing people in a multitude of countries. Her team was spread throughout Canada, the US, Israel and the UK, adding layers of managerial complexity to an already demanding position.

What Lily really enjoyed most was connecting with customers and working closely with them, coming up with creative solutions that would benefit them. She was at her best when she could connect on a personal level, leveraging her naturally playful personality and allowing for room to explore several options for solutions.

One of the things that I learned about Lily is she had a lot of doubts about playing big. She was also a lone player, the type who believes she can do everything herself. But at the level her new title afforded, doing it all by yourself isn't optional. You need teams working with you. You need to delegate tasks and coordinate people in different departments and regions to meet deadlines. For her, it was easier to do things herself rather than assign tasks or projects to the people she managed.

This is one of the leadership transitions that Ram Charan talks about in chapter two titled "From Managing Self to Managing Others" from his book, *The Leadership Pipeline*. Lily was feeling comfortable doing things herself, but like the rest of us, she had only 24 hours in a day. Even though she was sometimes working 16-18 hours a day, she didn't have the capacity to complete everything on her to-do list herself.

Here's where I helped her see the benefits of adopting elements of the Samurai and the Vinci. The Samurai could help her get a clearer sense of her core values, while the Vinci could help her trust the delegation process.

After we worked together, her performance with her team improved. She started delegating and both her confidence and gravitas increased. She started to command the room instead of succumbing to imposter syndrome and thinking, "Who am I to be a global leader?"

True to Samba fashion, Lily was often distracted by the next shiny object to come along, never wanting to invest the time into mastering any one thing. Unlike a Vinci, her reason for coming up with new marketing ideas was merely to satisfy her insatiable need for variety rather than sticking to one thing and seeing it through to its end.

But the promotion put her on a different playing field where, although her ability to improvise and adapt still mattered, she needed to become more disciplined around delegation and trusting others to get things done instead of taking it all on herself.

Unfortunately, despite the improvements I saw in Lily, she ultimately did not fully commit to the assignment. Any type of solution my team provides needs the full buy-in and collaboration from our clients and, in Lily's case, we could not continue because Lily decided to pursue other ventures. In many ways, this lack of commitment demonstrates perfectly the Samba persona in that a Samba is often looking for her next fun, shiny experience. While that playfulness and sense of fun adds tremendous value in certain roles, the position Lily acquired through her promotion demanded she improve her skills and add key elements of both the Samurai and the Vinci to truly succeed.

People who are predominantly Samba make for great:
- Marketing Managers
- Human Resource Managers
- Counselors
- Trainers
- Product Demonstrators
- Sales Directors

When I'm teaching people about the Samba persona, I use my hands to recreate a wave motion, undulating gently in front of me. This is the Samba power pose. Being in the moment and being okay with it are hallmarks of the Samba – so are smiling and a certain way of moving, like water flowing naturally across the land with no particular agenda except to eventually end up where it ends up.

The Samba persona is flexible in all ways, ready to change her direction on a dime. Her emotions are easily influenced by her surroundings; a change in music or what she observes can affect how she feels. Her empathy is strong, too, and she picks up the energy of those people around her more quickly than the other two personas. It would not be rare to find a Samba crying while watching a long-distance phone commercial that plays on emotions like love and happiness. For a Samba, separating her emotions from those on the screen is hard.

The Samba knows she's different than others because she picks up inspiration everywhere she goes. She loves that about herself. Even her breath varies depending on what is going on around her. She will most likely breathe from the lungs, more shallowly and lightly as doing that makes changing directions quickly easier.

The Samba's walk has a bounce to it; she swings her arms loosely at her sides without needing to control them. Gravity and momentum carry her along and she's not concerned about what others might think.

To see a video demonstrating the Samba power pose, visit **www.toyamaco.com/ssvbook**

Whereas we saw in the last chapter that the Samurai forms a straight line between point A and point B (remember the Samurai power pose), the Samba is curvy all the way. Both personas are purposeful, but what's driving the respective purposes is very different.

I will address that idea later in the book, but for now, let's look at what makes a Vinci tick.

Chapter 15: The Gift of the Vinci

When I was growing up, my father traveled a lot. He worked for the Ford Motor Company, and had to go to Detroit regularly. On one of his trips to the United States, he bought a LEGO kit for me. I was eight or nine years old at the time, and that kit was magical. We did not have LEGOs in Brazil; we had something called Playmobil.

The pieces that come in a Playmobil set are much bigger and not as refined as LEGOs. The kit my father bought me was the Galaxy Explorer set in which the figurines wore space helmets. This was very cool to my eight-year-old self because we had nothing close to anything like LEGOs in Brazil. We certainly didn't have little men wearing space helmets! Almost instantly, I recognized I had a hold of something very special.

I was already exhibiting entrepreneurial tendencies by this time in my life, so I came up with an idea to rent the little LEGO man with the helmets to kids at my school. I would rent him out at every single class. This venture turned out to be wildly successful.

I ran my little LEGO enterprise for a couple of years. I can still remember seeing kids in the class playing with that LEGO figurine inside their desk. They'd take his helmet off, then put it back on. They didn't play with any other parts of the kit -- just that little man.

I don't remember how much I made, but it was quite a lot.

Another venture I started in school was selling little booklets I made by stapling paper together and drawing Mickey Mouse or some other image on the front cover. People loved these little books and bought them. I also sold sheets of mica I got from a place my family went to about an hour and a half away from São Paulo where an entire hill of mica was there for the mining. Mica is glittery and glossy, and one of its properties is it peels off in little, shiny, glittery sheets.

I would collect many mica sheets and then sell them at school to kids in my class. Boy, did they love it. I did all this between the ages of eight and eleven. That was the Vinci part of me. I was a visionary. I was futuristic, always thinking ahead. I saw needs and gaps in the marketplace and fulfilled them. I even created new business categories!

However, a true Vinci knows how to communicate his vision to others and get buy in. I picked up this insight the hard way when I was in high school and missed out on a multi-million-dollar opportunity because I did not know how to communicate my idea effectively. It's one thing to be visionary, but it's another thing altogether to be visionary and know how to communicate that vision to stakeholders.

During my tenure in high school, I noticed the students needed a snack bar. I went home one day and told my father, "I'm going to start a snack bar at school" to which he quickly replied, "Are you crazy? No, you're not."

Based on my father's response, I immediately decided not to pursue my idea. I didn't go to my room and map out my big vision that I could share with him later that night. Instead, I allowed his doubt to stamp out my vision like a boot crushes a burning cigarette.

Turns out, someone else had the same idea for a snack bar. A few months later, he launched his version of the snack bar, and then a few years later, he launched a restaurant based on its concept because he made so much money. Then, from the restaurant, he launched a franchise and ultimately became a multimillionaire.

It's painful when something like that happens to you. Knowing that I could have been the one to make tons of money, start a restaurant and build a franchise still makes me think about what could have been. But like I said, I learned a very valuable lesson. Being able to communicate your vision is as important, if not more so, than the vision itself.

I sometimes wonder how my life would be different had I launched that snack bar before he did. I've always had the ability to see things happening long before they do. But in the snack bar situation, I did not have the communication skills to deliver it.

The Vinci persona originates from the master of innovation himself, Leonardo da Vinci. As my LEGO story illustrates, the gift of the Vinci is rooted in creative thinking, entrepreneurialism, and exploration. It also requires the ability to communicate the vision that evolves from those processes. This next story illustrates how that can work.

We were called to work with the senior director of a biotech company headquartered in The Netherlands, with operations on six continents and with sales of nearly €4 billion a year.

Paul had been the executive director of an American company that was bought by a Dutch biotech company. He is a natural Vinci-style person as he is very curious and passionate about his area of expertise, always eager to learn more about it and frequently exploring other areas of knowledge that could be useful and help him innovate.

He was struggling with the new culture, how projects were done and the new budget constraints. In his previous company, he'd had more autonomy, while in the new company, he did not have carte blanche or the necessary clout to influence his superiors, some of whom were based in Europe. Most importantly, problems with miscommunication were rampant, leading to too many misunderstandings with some team members and bosses working locally as well as in Europe.

To find out what was really going on, we suggested a solution that encompassed three phases.

In the first phase, we ran:

a) a Leadership Profile assessment (in this case, the Leadership Circle Profile™) to understand the skills and competencies that Paul was already good at and that we could help reinforce and the skills and competencies that he could improve upon;

b) as part of this first step, we also ran one-to-one interviews with his bosses, peers, and direct subordinates so we could understand the situation from their points of view; and,

c) with the input from the leadership assessment and the one-to-one interviews, we produced and distributed an online questionnaire to help measure the current levels of perception on how Paul was doing in the two key areas that we identified needed to be worked on: leadership and communication skills. The data was then analyzed and summarized in a report that formed the basis for the solution.

Phase two had us looking at the insights gathered from phase one so we could co-create and implement a plan of action with a step-by-step approach that involved executive coaching and a planned training curriculum including books, articles and thought leadership papers. This plan of action was shared with Paul, his boss and the HR manager so that every interested party could follow along and keep Paul accountable. This phase took about eight months and involved executive coaching sessions every two weeks, with supplemental reading materials in between.

Half-way through the process, we sent a quick email to the same people who were interviewed at the beginning of the process and asked questions related to whether they had seen a difference in Paul's leadership and communication skills. We asked for their input about what else might benefit his development. We then collated this information and, prior to implementing it, we shared it with Paul and his boss.

The third phase was a post-engagement measurement to determine the effectiveness of the solution. In this measurement, we compared the pre-and post-data and the results were very positive. The company saw a 420% ROI on their investment in executive coaching and training and a 21% increase in Paul's leadership skills, among other improvements.

After this process, Paul expressed how grateful he was to have gone through it. He said, "Claudio is an excellent executive coach. I benefited tremendously from his experience, insight, and individualized attention. He brought many new distinctive skills to my repertoire, including those of the SSV Way™. With the help of Claudio's coaching, I was able to advance my communication and leadership skills and lead my team to incredible successes. The results were tangible with clear, positive feedback from executives and staff."

People who are predominantly Vinci make for great:
- Art Directors
- Filmmakers
- Graphic Designers
- Creative Directors
- Lead Designers
- Product Managers
- Writers

When I'm demonstrating the Vinci power pose, I extend my right hand out from my body as if I'm pointing at an imaginary clock at the two o'clock spot. My fingers are extended and my arm is straight. I turn my gaze to look out at the horizon of possibility beyond that clock, imagining all the wonderful inventions and creative projects just waiting to be started.

The Vinci's posture is tall but not rigid. Her spine is strong; her extremities remain relaxed and fluid, representing her openness to possibilities. Her breath is steady – not overly deep, not overly shallow – and her demeanor remains even-keeled so that she she can see everything she needs to see.

Unlike the Samba, the Vinci doesn't automatically take on the ideas/emotions of others. Rather, she considers whether or not those idea/emotions are best for her and then decides if she should embrace them. She has a wide gaze, seeing all around her as well as beyond her horizon. She keeps a watchful eye open to what could improve her already well-thought-out plan. She is open to the ideas of others, but is picky about which ones she ultimately selects.

The Vinci's walk is strong but open. Her steps are shorter than those of the Samurai, but still in a straight line because she knows, in general, where she wants to end up. The Vinci is the regalest of the three personas; just as a Queen walks through her kingdom admiring the work she has done, absorbing the success she has created, and looking for areas to improve, so, too, does a Vinci approach her work and life. She celebrates beauty, innovation and a job well done, and she gets excited to see her ideas come to fruition.

To see a video demonstrating the Vinci power pose, visit **www.toyamaco.com/ssvbook**

Chapter 16: The Gift of the Samurai Samba Vinci Leader

So how do we recognize somebody who's got the SSV magic? What does a Samurai Samba Vinci leader look like? What happens when we put the three profiles all together to form the Samurai Samba Vinci leader?

For starters, an SSV leader behaves a certain way. It's the being piece at work. Who are they being out in public? For example, when they are in a restaurant, how do they treat the service staff? When they are in a professional setting, how do they treat those people who cannot help them advance their career and move up the ladder?

Secondly, an SSV leader inserts herself seamlessly into new situations. Her self-confidence is high and she trusts herself to execute accordingly. Lady Diana is a perfect example of an SSV leader because no matter what kind of situation she was in, she was always being her truest self and leading from an authentic place.

One thing I've heard from clients again and again is that when they are practicing the Samurai Samba Vinci Way™, they notice that they are treating other people with more respect, including people they may have overlooked in the past, like the person who cleans the company bathrooms. When you practice the SSV Way™, you will notice these kinds of differences in yourself, too. You're going to treat every person as a human being, not as someone who is beneath you because his or her job isn't glamorous or he can't do something for you. You will feel more at ease in new situations because you have solidified your core, made room for play, and created a space for considering new ideas without judgment.

According to Rolf Jensen and Mika Aaltonen in their book, *The Renaissance Society*, "Leadership dilemmas don't change; they are more or less eternal." In other words, no matter where we go in the world, or when we go there, leaders are facing the same range of problems. Some of those eternal problems include loyalty (e.g. who leaders are committed to within a company or organization), hierarchy (e.g. how companies are shaped and where information comes from), and value (e.g. how human capital is performing and at what level they are engaged). While the conditions in which dilemmas arise will change, the fundamental nature of those challenges remains the same.

Given this truth, the gift of the Samurai Samba Vinci leader becomes clear. For starters, a fully actualized SSV leader will demonstrate for those in her charge a strong set of core values while remaining flexible in a rapidly changing environment. She will see opportunities in new ideas and remain open to exploring them, even if they aren't within her area of expertise. She will value people for who they are and work with individuals as individuals, honoring their strengths and acknowledging their contributions to the team. She will show up consistently and make good on her promises because she frames and explains them accordingly. She will facilitate and coordinate rather than dictate and confuse.

In our globalized economy, uncertainty is a given, not a possibility. Remember the chapter on VUCA (Volatility, Uncertainty, Complexity and Ambiguity)? Uncertainty is always by a leader's side. Because the first priority of leadership is to engage the right people, at the right times, to the right degree in their work, an SSV leader will work with uncertain conditions rather than fight against them, or worse – try to change them.

Most leadership books don't talk about the range of predicaments leaders face, choosing instead to zero in on one dimension of being a leader. Is it any wonder new leaders are left with more questions than answers about how to solve problems?

When we think of world-class leaders, certain names always come to mind. Justin Trudeau. Elon Musk. Sir Richard Branson. Arianna Huffington. Sheryl Sandberg. These are examples of Samurai Samba Vinci leaders. What gives these people the designation and distinction of that title?

That's one question that took me decades to answer: These leaders personify the SSV Way™. It is not about performing at the highest level of one persona or another; it is about combining the gifts of the three personas. We need to be able to draw on the gifts from all three to earn that distinction. We need to be able to assess a situation and determine which elements, which flavors if you will, are needed to find the perfect recipe for success. Those leaders have mastered this piece of leadership.

If you work for a company that is more Samurai, for example, learn to be a little bit more Samba and Vinci. Be willing to ask, what are we going to need to learn to be more Samba and Vinci? If you are too much of a Samba in a culture that is a lot of Samba, how can you become more Samurai so that you can play on the bigger stage? If you're just Samba, Samurai, or Vinci, you're not going to be able to play at the world-class level.

In Brazil, depending on the school, if you don't earn a 7 out of 10 on exams and assignments, you don't pass in that discipline, and you must have at least a 7 in all disciplines to advance to another year. The same can be said of the SSV Way™. Even if you score lower in the other profiles, you can still achieve a certain level of awareness of the others so that you can succeed in your new leadership role.

This is what it takes to play in the same league as the Buffets and the Gates of the world. When you can stand in your strength from your core with unwavering self-awareness; when you can adapt without compromising from your core; and when you can remain open to new ideas and possibilities, you can consider yourself to be among the most elite leaders on the planet. Cultivating the gift for yourself is invaluable. Sharing the bounty of that gift with your organization is the ultimate reflection of your competency, and complements any company with which you are or will become affiliated.

Chapter 17: The Greatest Gift of All

For years I thought I wanted to become an aeronautics engineer when I grew up. That career path seemed as good as any as a gateway to seeing the world and also being around planes. I imagined entering this line of work for a long time. Then, for many different reasons, I did not.

While I occasionally think about how different my life would be today had I chosen that path, I'm very happy with what I do. I love that I get to work with people all over the world, helping them understand themselves better through the lens of the SSV Way™. I love experiencing different cultures. And because I travel as much as I do, I see a lot of airplanes up close and personal.

In my travels, I've discovered many things about people. For instance, while no two people are alike, we are all part of the human family. Some things are the same no matter where you go in the world, like the principles of mathematics and science. Two plus two equals four whether you live in Los Angeles, Buenos Aires, Cairo or Moscow.

But leading people? That's a completely different story! There is no universal formula for how to work with people. It's fascinating. We have seven billion people on the planet who are very different, yet at the same time, very much alike.

Hard sciences are, in some ways, easier to grapple with than soft sciences. Numbers are plugged into equations and things add up. Predictability is higher. Logic rules the roost.

The soft sciences, on the other hand, have so many more variables than the hard sciences. Emotion replaces logic in most cases, and deciding how to effectively and systematically interact with people in a VUCA climate can be difficult. Unlike physics -- where you can solve for the friction two cars create when driving toward each other from opposite directions -- no such simple formula exists for working with people. We can't plug individuals into an equation and come out with a duplicatable answer.

When leading people, variables include:
- What is their perception of me?
- What conversation did they have two minutes ago?
- Where are they coming from?
- What mood are they in?
- What is their personal history?
- What are their aspirations?

These variables factor into the leadership equation, so there is no one answer!

When I'm working with clients in an SSV capacity, I basically serve as a translator. With individuals who are heavily Samurai, for example, people who have mastered some area of expertise -- whether it's knowledge or art or cloud-based computing -- I'm able to affirm for them that they already have a solid Samurai base. What's missing are elements of the other two profiles. I then coach them to bring out elements of the Samba and the Vinci so they become more rounded and continue to stand tall in their mastery, while simultaneously communicating it, effectively expressing themselves, and connecting with others.

The SSV Way™ can extend beyond people and represent companies and countries, too. For instance, Brazil's economy and culture are heavily Samba. While this is good for some things, they could use a dose of Samurai for others. As of the writing of this book, for instance, "Operation Carwash" is underway in Brazil. It involves billions of dollars in bribes, corrupt government contracts, and a hefty serving of racketeering. Additionally, Brazil's most recent president was impeached, and its current president is allegedly corrupt. As executives at top companies are jailed for corruption, the workforce suffers with a tremendous loss of jobs. As if all this wasn't enough, Brazil is recovering from the worst depression in its history. Some Samurai mastery could certainly help here.

Japan, of course, has the Samurai ingrained, but with some Vinci as well. You'll see a blend of that in different countries, including the United States. For instance, the United States' culture has different elements at work depending on which region you visit. On the East Coast, for example, the prevailing culture has a staccato feel -- stop and go, stop and go, stop and go. The fluidity and playfulness of the Samba isn't present the way it is in southern California, for example, or other states closer to Mexico like Arizona and parts of Texas. Latino cultures tend to be more fluid and Samba-like.

Sometimes when you are part of a culture, it's very difficult to be anything but your dominant persona. I grew up in Brazil and lived there until I was 25. I was Samurai and Samba and Vinci, but not all at once. My friends made fun of the Samurai in me, but my father respected it highly; my father made fun of the Samba in me, but my friends loved it. Because of these potential conflicts between who you are and what culture you live in, questions can arise including:

- What are the expectations of where I live with respect to the SSV Way™?
- How can I be a Samurai in a culture that is primarily Samba?
- Can I be more of a Samba in a company culture that is more Samurai?
- How do I adapt?

Sometimes you cannot. Sometimes you're going to have a difficult time trying to fit in. You may need to assess within yourself what's preventing you from feeling fully aligned.

When a clash occurs between the profile of a company leader and the ethos of the company itself, we see a nice dance occur. Sometimes a leader can be more Samba working for a Samurai company. Sometimes the reverse is true. To recap, who you are being for a Samurai is grounded in self-awareness and knowing your core; in flexibility and playfulness for a Samba; in creativity and a spirit of innovation for a Vinci. The ultimate goal is to have the capacity and wisdom to draw on all three.

As you will discover in this next section, equations become irrelevant once you know your core and apply the principles of the SSV Way™. Understanding what makes you tick and what triggers you will free you up from forcing yourself to fit in. Essentially, the need to fit in will no longer exist. Because you now know yourself in an SSV capacity, you will be able to adapt to any situation effortlessly. If you are working with someone who is shaped like a star, you can adapt to their needs and become like a star without losing yourself.

Because of our inherent differences, there is a quest to create ways of understanding ourselves and one another so that we're not overwhelmed by the complexities of how different we are. That's the paradox of life.

I have witnessed time and again how people around the world fall into the three profiles outlined in this section. While we all have elements of each persona within us, in my work, I have learned that each of us tends to be fundamentally one over the other two. A fully actualized Samurai Samba Vinci leader will embody traits from all three, drawing her strength from what the immediate situation demands of her. Learning about the gifts each persona offers can help readers achieve that level of leadership, and ultimately, guide us closer to understanding the most important person of all in our lives: ourselves.

Now let's look at several practical applications for putting your SSV profile to good use.

PART III:
PRACTICAL
APPLICATIONS

Chapter 18: An Anthropological Approach to Leadership

Becoming an SSV leader is a lot like heading out into the wilderness on an adventure the way Indiana Jones did in the movie Raiders of the Lost Ark. The journey includes experiencing a transformation as we move from our previous role into our new one.

Indiana Jones transformed himself from a college professor (aka subject matter expert) into an international leader when he was commissioned to complete an archeological adventure. Tested time and again on his quest to find the Ark of the Covenant, Indiana had to rise to each new challenge and simultaneously draw on his innate strengths while channeling new parts of himself to not only survive life-and-death situations, but also accomplish the task with which he was charged. Our journey into leadership is very similar.

Just as Indiana used his whip to help him enter caves and overcome challenges on his search for ancient artifacts, leaders can use the SSV Way™ to unearth treasures living inside us to become better. Armed with our new knowledge from taking the Samurai Samba Vinci profile assessment, we can now begin to use that information to form a deeper understanding of ourselves via practical applications. Our experiences will eventually reveal a clearer picture about how we lead best. Remember: the SSV Way™ is a tool for helping us understand who we are being when we lead. Discovering how to use that tool is the focus of this chapter.

The first and arguably most important use of the tool is for building a strong foundation with an emphasis on improving our mindset, knowledge, and body awareness. As I've stated several times already throughout this book, having a strong, unflappable core will help you immensely on your leadership development journey.

When I begin working with new clients, we always start with building a strong foundation. I have discovered that almost everyone who has risen to a position of leadership already has part of their foundation in place. My job is to help pour concrete into the cracks and fill in any gaps, making what is already solid unbreakable.

Once we know what we stand for, adapting to the variables of a VUCA world as leaders becomes much easier. Remember in an earlier chapter when I talked about transforming into the shape of a star when working with a star-shaped person? This is but one of the many payoffs we enjoy when we ensure our foundation is indelible.

The most effective way to start the journey is to take a series of additional assessments (if you haven't already) that will give you insights into the nuances of how you think, make decisions, communicate and function in various situations. These assessments will shore up your mindset about yourself as a leader. Remember that awareness creates choice. I explore in detail several of my favorite assessments in chapter 29.

To understand ourselves better as leaders, we must also consider the five main ways our bodies "think." They are: flexibility, centeredness, stability, determination and openness. The way that we hold energy in our bodies determines our disposition toward approaching life's challenges. This part of my work is directly influenced by the Newfield Network, where I was trained and certified as a coach. The Newfield Network is grounded in a rigorous and substantive theoretical framework—known as ontology, defined in the dictionary as the branch of metaphysics dealing with the nature of being.

Being centered can be described best as being neutral. When centered, we are grounded and aren't swayed by the other dispositions or emotions. Think of a stick shift on a manual automobile. Just as we must move the shifter through neutral before changing gears, we must also move through center when changing from one emotion to another. Consider how difficult it would be to move from rage to joy – practically impossible. We must first get centered and grounded, then tap into our core before having the ability to see all our possibilities and ultimately choose which gear will be most advantageous to us.

Being determined is like having tunnel vision. We have one destination. We know how to get there. We know our way is the best way. We can lead with strength and power. We are not open to other points of view as this is not the time to do so. Things are urgent and must be taken care of quickly and efficiently. This is the stance a firefighter takes when rescuing someone from a fire. He does not ask the victim which way to go or what to do; he just does his job and demands that others follow his lead as he knows it's the best possible way and their lives depend on it.

The determination posture has one foot in front of the other with that same arm forward. This stance is like warrior 2 pose in yoga, but with the feet much closer together for stability while leaning forward slightly to show forward motion. When determined, we lean into what we know we are doing next. Our gaze is narrowed as if we have blinders on and we are focused only on the end goal. The breath is deep, but coming more from the lungs than the belly.

Being stable means being unmovable. Stability is like determination in that you know what is right at the core and you are not looking for input from others. In both dispositions, your beliefs are cemented and other people's opinions don't matter. The difference, though, is that being stable means that you have a much wider vision. When stable, you take in the whole picture. You have created something wonderful, you know it, and you are proud of it.

The posture for stability is one of strength and confidence. Feet are shoulder-width apart, arms are down at your sides, the spine is elongated, and the chin is parallel with the ground. The breath of stability is deep, slow and strong into and out of the diaphragm. The gaze moves slowly from one side of the horizon to the other, soaking everything in. Imagine a king high on his hill, looking over his kingdom with pride at what he has built with satisfaction and strength.

Being open is also a disposition that takes in the broad picture. When we are living in a state of openness, we welcome the opinions of others. We know where we are going and we have a strong idea of how to get there, but we also realize that others may be able to come up with a better way. We allow others to share their ideas, especially when we believe they will improve on our core idea. Leaders who have a plan in place, but still consider alternative ways to improve on it use openness to move forward with their idea. They know that accumulating the ideas of others will result in the best possible plan to accomplish goals.

The posture of openness has our feet just a bit further than shoulder-width apart, arms wide open but slightly in front of us as if we are reaching out for a big hug from a group of people. The chin is slightly higher than parallel to the floor and the eyes are softened. Our breath is deep in and out of the diaphragm as we inhale all the energy around us. We know what we want and welcome others to help us on developing the best way to get there.

Being flexible is a bit different. Some people have a difficult time differentiating between open and flexible. Like the open disposition, flexibility considers information from others. What differentiates it is its willingness to ditch everything previously planned when something better comes along. Being flexible means not having any preconceived notions as to what is going to happen. Being flexible is like going to a night club and dancing to every single song no matter what the song is. Fast, slow, familiar, new, techno, or country – none of that matters. With flexibility, switching gears just as quickly as the music changes is a given.

The posture of flexibility is the absence of a fixed posture. Flexibility is fluid and constantly moving. Arms are swinging every which way, legs are taking on different shapes, and the spine keeps twisting and turning. Our gaze is all over the place. Anything that catches our eye is what we will look at. In lieu of taking on a posture and holding it to practice the disposition, you continually change your posture to improve flexibility. The easiest way to do this is to change the music you are listening to and alter the way your body moves with each song.

If you'd like to incorporate any of these dispositions into your life, practice the pose explained for the one(s) you're interested in as described above. You can even meditate in a particular pose and see what comes up for you when you do.

These five main dispositions help us understand what our natural tendency is when reacting to challenges. For example, a Samurai leader can be resolute and want to plow through a problem as directly and quickly as possible. Underlying his determination is an attitude of "get out of my way." Samurais tend to possess high levels of determination.

A leader who scores higher on the Vinci profile might respond to a challenge along the lines of, "Oh okay. That's good. Let's move along this way, let's move along that way." Vinci leaders are known for being open-minded, trafficking primarily in the realm of possibility.

Samba leaders, who bring an air of "let's go with the flow" to the table, can sometimes be perceived as a pushover; they can get "run over" more often than Samurais or Vincis. Flexibility can be misunderstood, perceived as spineless rather than relaxed. However, being a pushover has less to do with flexibility and more to do with not having cemented our core values. When we are stable, when we are grounded, we become powerful leaders no matter what our primary persona is.

Sometimes when I ask my clients, "Do you think you are more resolute or more open?" they think that they're both. Then, when placed into situations to test their ways of being, they often will veer toward one or the other.

Developing our awareness of the five body dispositions enhances us as SSV leaders. Even though we may have a tendency or preference for one over the others, it's possible to learn how to incorporate the other elements into our leadership style. The beauty of developing a keener sense of our physical beings is twofold: 1) when we know what's missing, we can take steps toward closing the gaps and 2) it gently leads us to asking ourselves important questions including:

- How do I bring more determination into my life so that I'm more balanced?
- How do I bring more stability into my life?
- How do I bring more openness into my life?

Having a clear, complete picture of both competencies that help create the results we want and tendencies that limit our leadership potential are important to our growth. Participating in this type of information gathering through introspection and assessments is critical to our success as leaders in much the same way as market research is a critical component of business strategy.

I've been in market research for a long time and I have seen the pendulum of research styles swing over the years. The newest market research methodologies employ elements of ethnography and ethnomethodology. Ethnography is an inconspicuous method of studying how humans live as a means of discovering the link between behavior and culture and how this changes over time. Ethnomethodology concerns itself with the ways people respond to their environment considering their society's shared knowledge and reasoning. It seeks to describe the methods used in the production of social order. When applied to learning about what consumers buy and why, these approaches can lead to creating innovative products and services.

These research methods are popular right now because observing people in their natural environments seems to provide the most authentic data about human behavior compared to other research methods. This approach not only asks consumers questions about whether they would use Product X, but also observes them using Product X and asks them how they could see themselves using it. When interacting with the product, are they talking about themselves, or are they talking about the bigger social and cultural picture in which the product exists?

One common question a product researcher might ask is, "How would you behave under situation X or situation Y using this product?" Most consumers might answer, "Oh yes, I would be cool and gathered, no problem." But when placed in a real situation with Product X, the outcomes can be quite different than what was speculated in a controlled setting.

Leaders can employ similar strategies to uncover clues about how they might respond to variables in different professional settings. Case studies, workshop trainings, and role-playing exercises can introduce leaders to new concepts. Leaders can then explore the connections they see between who they once were as subject matter experts with who they are becoming in their new leadership role. One caveat to keep in mind is that too often we believe we will naturally respond to circumstances in the real world the same way we did with a case study in the classroom. How shocked so many of us are when we discover the real deal isn't as straightforward or simple to fix as the textbook intimated it would be!

Chapter 19: Developing Your Executive Presence

Executive presence has become a popular term in recent years. As the world of work races along a rapid trajectory of constant change, the need for leaders with executive presence has only grown. Executive presence is one of those things we sense someone has. When a person with it enters a room, we just feel it. Why is that important? Because people gravitate toward those individuals who have presence; they are the ones others want to work with.

Also known as gravitas, executive presence can determine our promotability factor, among other career related events. In fact, the Center for Talent Innovation, a nonprofit research organization in New York, discovered after surveying 268 senior executives for a study on executive presence that it counts for 26% of what it takes to get promoted.

But what exactly is executive presence and how do we get more of it?

In short, executive presence is the amalgamation of several elements including the ability to project gravitas. Gravitas includes things like confidence, decisiveness, poise under pressure, and stellar communication skills. Outward appearance is also part of the formula, and can go a long way to forming a positive perception of our level of executive presence with various audiences.

With the Samurai Samba Vinci Way™, people who are tapped for leadership roles can develop their executive presence to the point where audiences feel that you have it.

The following case study shows how I used the SSV Way™ to help a NASA Nobel Prize winner increase his executive presence and organize his communication style so his audience could relate to him.

John works for NASA Goddard Space Flight Center in Maryland, USA. He had heard about me and my involvement coaching TED Fellows, and was interested in learning how we could help him develop a stronger presence when speaking to different audiences.

In our first conversation, his curiosity about his subject matter was palpable. He told us that, given his Nobel Prize, he was getting invitations to speak all over the world. However, he felt that he could improve his stage and leadership presence, as well as the organization of his ideas and how to communicate in a way that was better tailored to the various audiences he addressed. Even if it meant that his speeches should be in layman's terms, he was game to making those changes.

He said, "I have a lot of content. I know a lot about my subject, but I'm not connecting with the audience. My presence is not strong. How can I make a much more impactful presentation?"

I have come to discover that people like John who have achieved tremendous success in their area of expertise are often incredibly humble. They recognize they are in the space of not knowing, and want to improve some aspect of their professional life. What holds them back more than anything else is their Samurai natures. In John's case, his deep knowledge of one highly specific subject area was the block.

We arranged to have our first meeting in a café relatively close to NASA Goddard Space Flight Center. John asked if he could bring his wife along and that turned out to be a terrific idea. Jane is a ballet teacher, more of a Samba relative to his Samurai. She attended several of our meetings, and that added a new dimension to the sessions as somatics and body posture are considerable influencers on how people perceive us (somatics is a field within bodywork and movement studies which emphasizes internal physical perception and experience).

We spaced these sessions in a way that he could initially process this information, practice the new skills in between sessions and then come back to learn the next step.

We met for several months, preparing him for his talks around the world and also helping him organize his first TEDx talk. He has grown as a speaker and has since given several TEDx talks that have delighted audiences.

We worked together using the SSV Way™, focusing on the structure of the presentation and engaging in storytelling. I asked him key questions including:

- What do you need to work on to have a strong presence?
- How do you need to present?
- How do you go through your presentation?
- How do you feel when you're presenting?
- How do you stand?

- Where is your core?
- What are your values?

I discovered his SSV foundation was a nice blend of Vinci and Samurai, so I wanted to help him build on those themes, while introducing a few elements of Samba.

We focused a good portion of our work together on his speech in terms of, "Okay, why are you saying this? Why are you saying that?" We collaborated on ways to make his content interesting (without being overly technical) for each persona who could be sitting in the audience.

He would generate many ideas and we would say, "Well, this one would not really fly," (which I found funny coming from someone who works for NASA), "but this one would. This is how you structure the presentation." Additionally, we worked on how to present those ideas so that they would connect to his own presence on stage. To achieve this, we employed a mix of elements primarily from the Samurai and the Samba profiles; the Samurai, for precision and accuracy; the Samba, for fluidity and movement on stage.

Overall, our solution involved working on three main aspects of his executive presence:

a) the selection and organization of appropriate themes to be presented
b) the essential elements for effective communication
c) his stage presence and body language

The results of working together speak for themselves. As part of our formal evaluation to measure the effectiveness of our process, John shared the following feedback:

"As a Nobel prize winner, I asked Claudio for help in communicating my science with the public. Claudio was exceptionally helpful in working with me to keep myself present and relaxed, being natural while being focused. He was brilliant on how to structure the presentations, how to understand what the audience would know or not know, how to make the presentations flow smoothly. I've now done four TED-style talks and I thank Claudio deeply for making them work well. I have more speaking engagements than I can count."

The number of invitations he has since received to present TEDx talks around the United States has only increased since working with me and the SSV Way™. His communication skills are sharper, and he presents information more clearly and on point. There is no question he has successfully developed his executive presence.

For people like John who are playing at a bigger level on a global scale, the playing field is different. Without gravitas, life will be extremely hard. Not only in terms of being pushed all over the place, but also for how audiences view us. Without gravitas, we won't command as much respect as those with it; we will also struggle internally with imposter syndrome, a condition in which we believe we don't belong in the role we have.

For instance, let's say that you're frequently traveling to different states, regions, and/or countries. Not only are you going to be exhausted physically, but if you're trying to mimic or become someone you're not because you think that's what success requires, you will flounder at best, fail at worst. Imitating someone else is like putting on a mask and pretending to be someone you aren't. But how can you be yourself without really knowing who you are or how to adapt to the demands of different cultures?

If you want to play at that bigger level (and even if you don't), your life can become much easier when you develop your gravitas. People will want to work with you. People will want to be around you. They gravitate around you. Gravitas, gravitate.

Because I recognize the SSV Way™ in myself as well as in others today, I am much more capable of having meaningful and impactful conversations than I was when I was first promoted. What's interesting is, as I've developed myself using the SSV Way™, people I work with tell me that I have that "certain something" that makes them want to work with me. This wasn't the case back in London when I was first promoted! In fact, to illustrate how ineffective I was in my new role, and how little gravitas I possessed I will share the story of a time when I cried in front of some direct reports.

We were letting one of the employees go and there was a heavy air of uncertainty in the company. I could see how worried people were. While I knew I needed to hold myself together as a leader, I also couldn't contain the emotion I felt for seeing this employee lose her job. I held an external meeting at a coffee shop off campus. I was the one who had to announce to my team that she was losing her job. Tears filled my eyes and members of my team witnessed me crying.

While crying was a perfectly human reaction to an emotional situation, I should have considered the impact of that reaction on my direct reports. I should have shown more fortitude to help my team face this adversity with courage. Regulating our own emotions to positively impact those we lead is part of having emotional intelligence (more on this in Chapter 21) which plays into our executive presence.

In the end, developing our executive presence is about finding, nurturing, and ultimately owning our authentic selves. It's replacing the statement: "I don't know who I am anymore because I have been trying to mold myself to this person" with "Okay, I'm here! Let's get to work!"

By making that one simple switch, anywhere you go, people can see and feel your gravitas because your energy is radiating from a different place. You will be shining so brightly, they won't be able to look away.

Chapter 20: Building More Trust with Your Teams

Trust is at the very foundation of every successful relationship a leader has with his team. For the SSV leader to perform effectively in today's VUCA environment, creating trust is essential. Because the SSV Way™ offers a way of understanding ourselves and others, we can use it to build trust with our teams. We can also use it to establish how the people on our team work, communicate and function effectively together.

Productivity suffers without trust, as does employee morale, retention, and the bottom line. A lack of trust can cause team members to feel apathetic, uncommitted and jaded, resulting in sabotaged workflows and stonewalled projects. In short, when there is no trust, productivity, employee engagement and innovation suffer.

Trust isn't automatically given with a new title. Just because we get promoted doesn't mean the people we are responsible for immediately trust us. Like anything else worthy of respect, trust needs to be earned. It takes time. It takes consistency. It takes knowing who we are in relation to the rest of the organization, and especially to our team, to foster a culture based in trust.

Before we receive trust, we must first give it. It is reciprocal. For our team to trust us, we must demonstrate to our team that we trust them. A leader who doesn't show that he trusts his team will not be trusted in return.

Finally, a big challenge for leaders working in large, complex organizations is building trust across barriers of distance, cultures, time zones, and technology. For those companies that use a matrix style of organization, for example, people have competing goals and multiple bosses which can complicate trust-building efforts of even the most skilled leader. At its most basic level, trust is first and foremost about relationships, based on our perceptions of people's words and action.

Building trust using the SSV Way™ is straightforward. Because building trust requires aligning our words with our actions, we can apply the core elements of each profile to what we say and do, always keeping our audience front and center.

Are you going to do what you say? This is a central question every SSV leader must be able to answer confidently. Your team is counting on you to follow through with what you say and to see you acting accordingly.

Building trust with others requires taking the time to really get to know them -- what makes them tick. Real trust can take a very long time to build, but it can be destroyed almost instantly.

In his book *The Thin Book of Trust*, author Charles Feltman talks about the four pillars of trust: sincerity, reliability, competence and care. As developing SSV leaders, we can glean critical insights from him about leading effectively.

"Sincerity," he writes, "is mean what I say, say what I mean and act accordingly. Reliability is, 'You can count on me to deliver what I promise.' Competence is, 'I know I can do this; I don't know if I can do that' and care is, 'We're in this together.'"

So how can we go about building more trust with each of the three personas?

Let's look at the task of producing a report. This type of request happens millions of time a day around the world. While it may seem simple and straight-forward to an outsider looking in, report production requires more trust than at first meets the eye.

A Samurai who has requested a report will expect it to have the exact number of pages designated and for it to arrive at precisely the time set.

A Samba who has requested a report will expect it to show up eventually and won't put too much stock into whether it has five pages or fifteen as long as the main ideas are covered adequately. A Samba will be okay if the report arrives an hour past the deadline because, after all, things do come up.

A Vinci who has requested a report will expect it to show some creativity and will be quite impressed if the report is presented with some added flair and attention to detail. While it's fine if the report is plain, a Vinci will gush over one that went above and beyond the call of duty to make it aesthetically pleasing as well as accurate.

Sometimes leaders can sound sincere when they are trying to get a project done, but they go on to not make good on their promise. They are sincere when they make the promise, but if they are more Samba than Samurai, for example, chances are good something else will come up, taking them in a different direction and therefore, not delivering on the promise. This can cause all sorts of problems, including delayed delivery of projects, general confusion, and compromised communication.

Let's say that you're a Samurai working with a Samurai. Samurais tend to take things seriously. They're going to be sincere; they're going to be reliable; they're going to be competent. If they're not competent at a task or skill, they're not going to admit that publicly. They will never volunteer, "Oh, I'm sorry, but I don't know how to do what you're asking of me." They are more prone to hide behind their subject matter expertise, saying instead, "Well, I'm the subject matter expert here, so I should know how to do this."

Sambas can sound sincere when they make a promise, but their reliability is something else altogether. If you work with Brazilians, for instance, you will discover some Brazilians are reliable while others are not. Of course, this can be said of people in any culture, but Brazil's collective Samba culture is particularly representative of this fun-first profile, which some people can perceive as unreliable.

As we've learned, the Samba leader is flexible. Commitments are not written in stone so commitments can change according to the whims of the Samba. "Oh, I have something else going on now, so I cannot make it to the event we originally planned." Their unreliability can negatively trigger the Samurai.

You see this behavior when asking for directions in Brazil. Approach a local about how to get somewhere and a typical response is, "Oh yeah, just go here, just go there, just go there," when actually they have no clue what they're talking about or how to get to the desired destination. They will simply tell you, "Oh yeah, just go and go."

In terms of care, one thing that I see in a lot of Samba-like people is that they really care. When they say something, they really care about what they've said, and there is that level of interpersonal connection. In general, the care is there. Of course, we have exceptions to the rule as well.

Vincis can be sincere, and they can be reliable. They may at times struggle with competence because they are spending too much time in the brainstorming quadrant. With a fierce drive to constantly innovate, Vincis can lose sight of time and never develop mastery in one thing the way their Samurai colleagues do. They want to produce something different, innovative or more creative.

Once we have a clearer understanding of someone's SSV profile, we can apply the four distinctions of trust and say, "Okay, so why is it that I'm not really trusting what Claudio is saying to me? Is it because he's not being sincere or is it because he's not being reliable? Is it because he's incompetent or is it because he doesn't care? What is it about the promise that he's making that is not congruent?"

Sometimes trust can be broken, not because people are being incompetent, but because they don't share the same priorities. Being on time is not a priority for a Samba, for example, but is for a Samurai. Consider a meeting between two people scheduled for 3 p.m. If one person is there at 3 p.m. but the other person arrives at 3:05, reliability may come into question for that Samurai. He may ask himself, "Can I rely on this person to deliver on the promise if they cannot even make a 3 p.m. appointment on time?"

For some people, being on time is basic. 3 p.m. is 3 p.m. They question why being on time is complicated for others. A mainland US company conducting business in Hawaii with local Hawaiians, for example, who have a Laissez-faire, Samba attitude toward punctuality, must learn this concept of "Hawaiian time" very quickly. Surf could be up; someone's auntie could need help preparing the Kalua pork for that evening's luau. These are perfectly acceptable priorities for Sambas. Regardless, leaders are ultimately responsible for preparing our workforce for these disparities. Doing so will not only deepen trust, but it will lead to other desired results like improved efficiency and a bigger bottom line.

Chapter 21: Creating a Sustainable Culture in Your Organization

How can the SSV Way™ help you create a sustainable culture in your organization?

Creating a sustainable culture in any organization is no easy feat. When thinking about sustainability, a fully actualized Samurai Samba Vinci leader needs to consider what the entire experience is like when anyone interacts with her company. Stakeholders in every corner need to be considered. That list includes the supplier's experience, the shareholder's experience, the employee's experience, the customer's experience, the vendor's experience, the environment's experience and the community's experience.

In the end, sustainability comes down to being conscious about all the stakeholders, not just the ones who are most convenient or obvious.

Questions about how we are impacting the environment, how we are impacting the communities, how we are impacting the people working with us are all part of the sustainability puzzle.

Throughout my travels, I have seen companies completely

destroy the natural environment around them. That's not sustainable. They are not only destroying nature, but they're also destroying local communities.

I've worked with companies who struggle with sustainability, and I've worked with companies who didn't want to address the common issues associated with having a sustainable model.

Companies like Costco and The Body Shop, whose conscious initiatives are well-known in business, set the bar high for other companies looking to create sustainable cultures. Costco, for instance, pays its employees above minimum wage which contributes to a lower turnover rate and higher profit margin than its competitors experience. That's sustainable.

The Body Shop is known for having a philanthropic foundation, helping its suppliers in remote locations to form business cooperatives so they earn a living wage while simultaneously protecting their local communities.

Regarding sustainability, SSV leaders need to ask the following questions: What's the bigger picture? Where are we focusing our time, talent and resources? Are we focusing on ourselves or on the bigger picture? It's one thing to say, "All right! We won the trophy!" but how are we going to use that win going forward to make a difference?

All organizations -- whether tiny or enormous, growing or downsizing -- face these questions. By focusing on the organization's core competencies, an SSV leader increases the odds of sticking around for the long term and continuing to provide value to all stakeholders involved.

Chapter 22: Putting People First with Emotional Intelligence

I still remember the first time I attempted to ask out a girl. Oh my God, talk about panic, panic, panic!

First of all, it took me eight months to get around to it. We were in school together and I needed all that time to muster up the courage to approach her. One day I noticed that when we passed each other on the stairs and in the school corridors, she was looking back at me when I was looking at her.

Inside, I felt like confetti was falling from the ceiling of my heart. I could barely contain the desire to shout, "Woohoo!" as I ran through the halls.

Outside, I was still terrified.

Finally, after those eight long months, I got up the nerve to talk to her. My voice was crackling and I was visibly shaking.

I said something like, "How are you doing?" but I honestly don't really remember the exact words.

Instead of talking to me, however, she turned to someone next to her and talked to them! I panicked so much that I just left. I never went back to talk to her again.

When anyone tells me that I am so good at talking to people

and have a natural knack for it, my response is always, "If only! I've had to learn those skills over many years and through a lot of practice."

Connecting with people on an emotional level can be difficult. I had to make a point of learning people skills and increasing my emotional intelligence quotient. Being a beginner, especially for experts, is hard to embrace. We're so used to being the star. We're so used to knowing everything about our topic. Suddenly, we're thrown into new situations and our brain sends off a million alarms. As a means of coping, we resort to assuming, well, I'm just going to keep doing what I've always done because I've been successful. This approach can be disastrous.

Research on emotional intelligence and its importance to personal and professional success has gained momentum in the last ten years. Discoveries about the ways our emotions impact our behavior are influencing organizations around the world. A 2015 FAST Company article reported that research done by The Carnegie Institute of Technology showed that 85% of our financial success was due to skills in "human engineering," personality, and ability to communicate, negotiate, and lead. They found that only 15% was due to technical ability. In other words -- people skills or skills highly related to emotional intelligence were crucial skills.

This wouldn't be a true 21st century leadership book if I didn't touch on how our growing understanding of emotional intelligence is shaping leadership development.

The beauty of using the SSV Way™ as a development tool is

by design, it has elements of emotional intelligence baked into it. Psychology Today defines emotional intelligence as:

"The ability to identify and manage your own emotions and the emotions of others. It is generally said to include three skills: emotional awareness; the ability to harness emotions and apply them to tasks like thinking and problem solving; and the ability to manage emotions, which includes regulating your own emotions and cheering up or calming down other people."

In short, emotional intelligence has to do with being smart about feelings.

As an SSV leader, being smart about your feelings as well as the feelings of those for whom you are responsible is critical. This is where mastery comes into play. With your strong core developed (Samurai), you not only know who you are, but you also know how you react to emotionally charged situations. Negative emotions like rejection and disappointment are inevitable; with your Samba at work, you won't create emotional baggage, choosing instead to travel lightly as you go with the flow. Your vision for what's possible (Vinci) will keep you and your team focused on the future, giving those with whom you work an opportunity to see beyond what's currently happening.

One of the most pervasive and prevalent emotions I see preventing people from achieving leadership greatness is disappointment. Disappointment occurs when reality doesn't match our expectations. When we assume everybody is like us, we set ourselves and our teams up for misunderstandings. Working by ourselves as the expert in our designated area, we are responsible for only managing ourselves. We can invest our time and energy into mastering the content of our expertise. If we want to grow a little bit bigger in the company, of course, we will be expected to present and interact with other people who may or may not understand what we do at the level we understand it. The higher up the leadership ladder we climb, the more influence we'll have over a greater number of people.

As far as disappointment goes, no one profile is more immune to its effects than another. However, I have witnessed that the more Samurai a person is, the more likely he will be disappointed when expectations aren't met. For some reason, people who love structure tend to be the most disappointed when things don't go as they thought they would.

This explains why I should not have cried in that coffee shop years ago when announcing to my team that a team member was being let go. I had not demonstrated emotional intelligence; I did not regulate my own emotions to encourage, comfort, or calm those who looked to me to do so. I was not smart about my feelings.

Questions arise at this point such as: How can we find more common ground, increase productivity, and reduce communication blocks? How can we show up at work and prevent backbiting and backstabbing so people can just do what they need to do efficiently like a well-oiled machine? How can we ensure the right people are consulted about projects in the manner that makes the most sense for them?

Backstabbing is a curious phenomenon to me. Most of what I have seen is unintentional. It doesn't originate from someone being mean or being a jerk. It comes from an unawareness of of the cause and effect relationship between our actions and the way they impact others. What was unintentional by one is viewed as backstabbing by another. That's another important nuance of cultures and corporate cultures: Sometimes the people within those cultures are clueless. It's not that they're trying to undermine our work or make us feel like a loser; it comes down to some people not being aware of how their actions impact others.

Misunderstandings happen not only at work, but when visiting foreign countries, too. It is well-known that, when visiting Rio, you're going to be talking to a lot of Cariocas. Cariocas are the people who live in Rio. They have a reputation for saying things like, "Oh yeah, come over for a barbecue!" and not following through on their word. To a Samurai, a statement like this is a promise; many of my foreign friends who visit Brazil will respond, "They always promise, but they never deliver." Actually, that's not true because from a Cariocas' perspective, what they said about coming over for a BBQ was a conversation for possibility, not certainty.

Unless they provide the address and say something like, "Come by on Sunday at 1 p.m. because we're going to have a barbecue at my house," then for them, that reference to coming over for a BBQ is merely chatter. Samurais tend to take everything at face value; if you say something about a BBQ, then it's going to happen. Whereas a Samurai's brain is programmed for logic and precision, a Samba's brain is like, "I don't even remember what I said two minutes ago, let alone last week when I tossed it out!"

Then the Vinci comes along and is somewhere in the middle. It's a little bit easier for Vincis to let disappointment roll off their back. There's also an element of, "Oh man, I thought that sounded like a great time. I'm sorry it didn't work out." But they're not devastated. What fascinates me about Samurais is, for not being emotional creatures, they tend to suffer the deepest wounds when things don't happen as they expected.

Sambas are most disappointed when too much structure is imposed on their free-flowing approach to living and working. If too many demands are put on Sambas, they will feel imprisoned and caged in. Vincis are most disappointed when their ideas aren't accepted or recognized.

Another example of emotional intelligence at play with the three personas is what I call "No Invitation." In this scenario, we can see how people respond to feeling left out. Here's a snapshot of what this scenario looks like.

Let's say a vice president tries to set up a new initiative in her company and does not involve one of the other vice presidents for no reason other than VP #1 sincerely believes it's not worth VP #2's time, that VP #2 is already super busy with other projects. Unfortunately, a perception exists that these two VPs are not getting along, so by VP #1 not inviting VP #2 to participate, VP #2 thinks, "Oh yeah, she really doesn't want me to get involved because she wants all the credit" instead of seeing it for what it is -- "I just didn't think of involving you at this stage." Not being invited to participate led to the perception of VP #1 undermining VP #2, when no such thing was ever intended.

To further complicate this situation, sometimes VP #2 can take the perception one step further and think, "You're not involving me because maybe you don't like me or because you don't want me to get any credit for it." Believe me when I say this kind of situation happens so often, you can put any name of any company and any title of any job and see this scenario playing out every day in organizations around the world.

How can the Samurai Samba Vinci Way™ help prevent this kind of misunderstanding from happening?

For starters, based on my observations of this scenario in motion, VP #1 is far more likely to be a Vinci or Samba than a Samurai. If they are a Vinci, they are more likely to be innovating—thinking about and playing with the different options; they're not going to be involving everyone before they have something a little bit more tangible. If she is more like the Samba, she is simply throwing ideas out there and just seeing what sticks and what doesn't -- just playing with it a little bit and not setting anything in stone. VP #2 can be any of the three personas, but she will most likely be more of a Vinci or Samurai than Samba.

What hurts most in this situation depends on the primary persona of the participants. If they're more of the Samurai, they're going to be hurt because, in their quest for mastery, they want to get exposed to different things. They may think, "Oh, maybe this is a new way of doing something that I haven't thought about" or "This is a more improved version of something, and I would love to know about it." By their natures, Samurais are on an eternal quest for mastery. By not being invited to particpate, they feel left out.

The Samba, because of their nature to get involved with as many different experiences as possible, , is thinking more along the lines of, "Oh yeah, I was not invited to the party." But the Samba is able to brush it off more quickly than the other two personas because he knows something else will come along soon.

Because the Vinci is on a quest for innovation, she might think, "Yeah, I could create different ways of doing things, and envisoining a different future." The Vinci's wounds stem from not having the chance to flex her creative muscles and potentially discover a breakthrough. When we understand the different ways the three personas think about and approach assignments, we can reduce the number of times feelings get bruised.

In almost every situation, no malice lurked behind the decisions. I've seen very few instances where one person was intentionally being nasty or trying to hurt another person on purpose. It was unintentional. They were simply unaware of how their action could be interpreted.

This is why a dedication to expanding our self-awareness through the Samurai Samba Vinci Way™ can make life at work smoother and more successful. People like to feel included. Once we understand our primary persona and how it relates to the other two, we can cater our communication style accordingly and begin to make disappointment a thing of the past.

Chapter 23: Delegation and the Five Elements

Leaders are responsible for delegation, and need to understand how to delegate effectively respective to the people to whom they are assigning tasks. A consistent challenge I see in my clients is making the leap from being assigned tasks by a superior to assigning tasks to direct reports.

The Institute for Generative Leadership has identified the five elements for making requests. They include:

1. Who is making the request and who is receiving it
2. Conditions of satisfaction
3. Specified time for fulfillment
4. The shared background of obviousness
5. Concern is clear – why is the request being made?

When we apply the five elements to becoming an SSV Leader, delegation becomes easier and more streamlined with greater results.

The first element revolves around the people involved in a request. Who is speaking and who is listening? Who is the performer of the request and who's the audience? This sounds rudimentary, but imagine a meeting in which one person says, "We need to do this project. We need to implement this system."

I've heard these vague and generalized requests made many times; the outcomes are rarely positive. Too much information is missing, leaving those with whom a request has been made scratching their heads and guessing.

A critical question for everyone involved here is: Who in the room of 20 people is the we that is going to be implementing the request? Is the performer identified? Is the customer identified? Too often, it's not. The person making the request needs to be super clear about who is assigned which specific tasks and responsibilities required to fulfill the request.

"John is going to be producing this wireframe and I'm going to be the one that is going to be checking on you to see if it is done," is one example. Another is. "John and Mary will be creating the copy for the new website. There is a team working on it. Adrian and April will be the customers for it."

The second element is the conditions of satisfaction. If a leader says, "Claudio, you need to produce a report by Friday this week," I might be thinking, "Okay, what is this report like? Is it a two-page report, a summary report or a 45-page report in detail? What conditions do I need to meet to satisfy the request?"

Too often, those specific details aren't expressed. I've heard versions of the following more times than I can count: "Claudio, can you produce this report for me by Friday?" Without any specifics, I'm left having to figure things out on my own – often with disappointing results because I didn't do things right. Expectations must be clear for the conditions of satisfaction to be met.

The third element is a specified time for fulfillment. Often, we listen to a request like, "Can you do this for me ASAP?" First of all, what does the request mean? Does it mean that I need to drop everything that I'm doing so that I can just focus on that straight away, or does ASAP mean that it can be done by tomorrow morning? Requests need to be very clear with a specific time for anticipated fulfillment.

In New York, for instance, ASAP means yesterday. In Brazil, it may mean in the next couple of months. In Italy, the same, or maybe in the next month or so after ferie d'agosto, August vacation when the majority of city dwellers head to the seaside or countryside for an entire month. (This time off and away is sacred to Italians and leaders would not ask or expect the work to be done during this time.)

An improved version would go something like this: "Claudio, I need this 10-page report done by 5 p.m. Eastern Standard Time on Friday the third." A request like that leaves no room for error, no room for misunderstanding.

The fourth element is the shared background of obviousness. Is what we are asking someone to do obvious or not? Sometimes, especially if we're working with multiple departments and matrix teams, the project's background is completely different. The people we are asking to help us have no clue what we're talking about. No shared background of obviousness exists.

It's important to make sure what we're asking is obvious not just in our department, but across all the channels involved in the request. Just because we have been working in a specialized area doesn't mean we can assume everyone else will understand what the task or project is about or what's being asked of them.

Without paying attention to all the players in a scene, too often the response can be something like: "I have no clue what you're talking about" or "My background is completely different."

The fifth element is the concern for the request. Why are we asking what we are asking for? Why is it that we need it? For example, "I need those reports because I'm going to be having a meeting with the shareholders on Saturday morning. That's why I need them done by 5 p.m. Eastern Time on Friday." Or, "What I need is a two-page executive summary because I'm not going to have time to read through the entire 45-page report before the meeting."

The concern for the request is very clear in these examples. The person making the request has addressed why this particular request is important.

Once all five elements exist in the request, the number of times that we need to go back to someone gets reduced significantly. I've worked with people who have had to go back to their teams 10, even 15 times because one or more of the five elements wasn't present. Delegation becomes a nightmare in these cases.

That happens quite a lot. One of my clients asked someone over the course of six months to produce something, but it was not produced. When we reviewed the elements of request and he applied them, the project got produced in less than one week. Greater clarity would have expedited this request.

When I hear people say, "I don't have time to go through all five elements," that old saying comes immediately to mind: "If you don't have time to do it right the first time, when will you have time to do it over?"

Regardless of your primary SSV persona, becoming masterful at delegation can save leaders a lot of time, frustration and confusion. It is also a skill that causes our direct reports to respect us more, increasing our executive presence and trust, too. Applying the five elements to our understanding of the SSV Way™ clearly improves the chances of requests being done properly, on time and with fewer misunderstandings.

Chapter 24: Common SSV Communication and Perception Pitfalls

I remember when I was looking for apartments in London. I arrived five minutes late to my appointment to see an apartment because there'd been a delay on the "tube" (London's nickname for its subway system). As I walked up to the unit, the guy who was going to show me the apartment was leaving.

I apologized for being late and he said, "I don't care. You were not here at 2 p.m." I said, "Could you just show me? I'm here now. It took longer to get here than I anticipated." He replied. "You should have planned to be here on time."

Initially, I felt he overreacted to my tardiness. Coming from Brazil where being five minutes late means you're still on time, I wasn't accustomed to the way British people perceive time. I would quickly learn, however, that being five minutes late to a Brit signifies a break in trust and suggests you are unreliable. I imagined the leasing agent thinking, "If he can't get to an appointment on time, will he be able to pay his rent when it's due?"

Most communication problems boil down to the perceptions of the respective parties involved in the communication. My apartment story showcases how both the leasing agent and I had different perceptions of time, which led to a loss for us both. I lost because I didn't get a chance to see the apartment. He lost because he didn't get a chance to close a sale with a new tenant for the space.

Even the best of us will face communication challenges in our day-to-day responsibilities. In this chapter, I examine some of the most common pitfalls the three personas encounter and how to overcome them.

But first, let's talk about the roles of framing and explaining in effective communication.

Framing is just like it sounds -- how we construct our communications. Just as a builder erects the frame of a new house to give it shape and structure, so too must leaders create our messages with proper scaffolding. Whether short or long, messages with a solid frame tend to cause fewer misunderstandings than those that aren't framed. Additionally, offering a reason or explanation with our message can add to its overall success.

For instance, when a manager promises something to her team, she needs to make that promise contingent upon specific future events. She might say, "We're going to get a new system for tracking leads if we get the funding at this level by the end of the year." Framing the promise with a date alleviates the common problem of general promises such as: "Oh yeah, we're going to get this new system." Should the funding not come through, people aren't surprised or disappointed with the former promise because the conditions were clearly established.

Unlike the latter promise, it is clear and grounded in specifics. That's the frame.

The second part to effective communication is the explanation. Psychological studies about people cutting in front of the line in banks and other public places where lines are common reveal insights about how explanations affect our perceptions. One study revealed three main responses to someone cutting in line.

In the first scenario, a person cuts in front of someone in line without an explanation. People in the line get really annoyed with the person who cut. In the second scenario, someone cuts in line and says, "Can I just cut in line here?" The overall response is mixed to this behavior: some people will say yes and some people will say no. Finally, when that same person cuts in front of the line and offers an explanation -- even if it isn't that great -- people are much more likely to let them cut in line without protest.

Let's look at a common communication problem at work involving email. The story is often the same. Someone sends an email to someone else, promising to deliver something to them by a certain date. Then, they don't. The original sender sends another email, and again, they don't reply. Now the original emailer is boiling.

On the third email, the sender is really angry, using strong language like, "If you don't get back to me by this date, it's all over! You don't get the project!"

Then, suddenly, a response.

The person writes, "I'm really sorry. My father passed away

and I was arranging the funeral. I couldn't think about anything else." That is the explanation. At this point, the original emailer is much more likely to let things go because the explanation is so strong. The angry emailer is likely thinking something along the lines of, "Oh my God, I'm really sorry for being such an ass. I was being very petty with my expectations here and this person just had a major event happening in their life." Obviously, this is not said out loud, but who among us hasn't had a thought like this running through our minds upon discovering we had completely misunderstood a situation?

In coaching, we talk about "conversations for possibility" versus "conversations for implementation." Sometimes we are just discussing possibilities, throwing ideas out, brainstorming. We are not in a conversation about implementing something. We need to be aware of the difference between the two and frame our conversations appropriately. If our purpose is not clear, someone will ultimately walk away from that conversation disappointed.

For instance, if one says to another, "Oh yeah, next week, let's go out and celebrate," that was a conversation for possibility. Someone who takes everything seriously may interpret that as, "But you promised we were going to be celebrating." It was just a casual comment made in passing, just a conversation for possibility. No time or date was set on the calendar; no meeting place was determined. Even if the above example was met with, "Okay, yeah, let's do that," it is still a conversation of possibility.

Being aware of the difference between the two types of conversations can prevent many misunderstandings, thereby building trust between two people and/or two organizations.

Chapter 25: Preventing SSV Triggers

I have enjoyed going to meetings since I was in school. For me, meetings are designed for people to address an agenda, solve problems and get things done. When a meeting is scheduled to begin at 3:00 pm, I want it to start at 3:00 pm. Not 2:55 pm or 3:05 pm -- 3:00 pm. This stems from the Samurai in me.

Sambas, as we've learned, like fluidity and can change course without warning. If something comes up for a Samba right before a meeting is scheduled at 3:00 pm, they don't think twice about not showing up at 3:00. They might roll in at 3:30, at 4:00, or maybe not at all. When pressed for an explanation, Sambas are known for saying:

"Oh, didn't you hear? We're not going to have this meeting anymore. We don't need this meeting because we had a conversation in the hall by the water cooler and the problem we were going to talk about is now solved."

This change is perfectly fine for Sambas, but for Samurais, last minute changes like this don't work well. Samurais don't like sudden change and they certainly don't have time to waste! Each persona will be triggered by things the other two personas do and say. One of the keys to becoming a successful leader is learning what triggers us and how to work through those triggers -- becoming more proactive versus reactive.

After going through the SSV Way™ myself to understand my values and myself better, I pinpointed what triggers me and put a plan together to help me avoid having them poked. Whenever I'm having a conversation and I get annoyed by what someone working with me is saying or doing, I know exactly why I'm getting annoyed so I can do something about it instead of disengaging and shutting down.

Common triggers include situations involving:

- Time
- Quality
- Productivity
- Engagement
- Follow through
- Respect
- Usefulness
- Beauty

Newly promoted managers can benefit from studying this list, in large part because it elevates self-awareness. If they are a subject matter expert and they are just working by themselves, that's one thing; they are an expert in one area. When they are managing people or working in teams, not having the self-awareness of what makes them tick and what doesn't and what triggers them and what doesn't can make things even more difficult. Self-awareness is the first trait new leaders need to develop.

Triggers can also be traced to how mastery is respectively defined for each persona:

Mastery for the Samurai is more about accuracy than just about anything else. It is about getting better and better at something in a very precise way.

Mastery for the Samba is getting really good at the basics, but perhaps more importantly, how a Samba uses the basics to break the rules and get away with it. They're recognized for being outlaws and revered for being that way because most people would never dare to push the boundaries as far as they do.

Mastery for the Vinci involves knowing what the parameters are and how to work successfully within them to innovate and create. What does success look like? In advertising, for example, you can be as creative as you want as long as you work within the certain formulas particular to adverts. Emotion, images and words need to be combined just right for the formula to succeed; otherwise, the campaign doesn't work and mastery isn't achieved for the Vinci.

As you can see, a person who is primarily Samurai will be triggered and annoyed by someone who is more Samba-like or Vinci-like because they're all over the place with their "let's play" and "let's innovate" cores. A Samba feels fenced in and restricted by a Samurai saying, "You must do it this way." Similarly, a Vinci feels pinned in by a Samurai, too, because a Samurai is rigid and a Vinci is not. I have been triggered by all three at one time or another, depending on which persona was dominant at the time.

If you are a Samurai, last minute changes to plans will trigger you and you will say, "No, no, no, that plan was not on paper. How can you do that?" Because a Samba is very fluid and flexible, last minute changes are no big deal and quite common.

When someone knocks on a Samurai's door at an unscheduled or unplanned time, his response will likely be something along the lines of, "Wait a minute, we don't have a meeting planned for this hour." Last minute changes or even people arriving late to meetings or not taking things too seriously will trigger the Samurai.

The Samba can feel constricted by the Samurai's way because she's about fluidity and flexibility. To a Samba, the Samurai is too regulated. Remember my example of driving in Brazil? The stop signs there are just a suggestion. Nobody stops at the stop sign; they just look both ways and go. There is no counting one-one thousand, two-one thousand, three-one thousand and then go. No—as you approach the stop sign, you look both ways; if no cars are coming, you just continue going. In some parts of Brazil, the red light is also a suggestion. This kind of a Samba mentality drives a Samurai crazy.

At the same time, if you are Samba-like and you have to follow the rules to a T, you will feel like you're losing your mind. For the Samba persona, when you are going with the flow, you don't want to stop, you just want to go. You don't want any rules or regulations to get in your way or hear anyone say, "This is the sandbox that you can play in." That's one of the many interesting nuances of the Samba.

The Vinci is also very interesting because he lives and breathes beauty and innovation. A painter, for instance, who wants to paint on a canvas has that delineated space where he can be very creative while working within the defined space of the canvas. If he approaches painting like a Samba, just doing whatever he wants, he won't have any kind of a frame or even a framework to work with. That's the interesting thing about the Vinci because to be creative, to be innovative, he needs to have some boundaries, he needs to have some guidelines along with the free flow.

There are leaders who fit this description and they've gone down in history. Steve Jobs is a good example because he had the attitude of, "I'm going to pursue this project until I get it right" which reflects the Samurai, but he also worked within boundaries to just keep innovating, innovating, innovating until he said, "Now, it's ready" -- traits of the Vinci.

One thing to keep in mind is the goal of this model is to help readers become a more complete being by drawing on the elements of all three personas. The Samurai is connected to discipline and the pursuit of mastery (which can take decades to achieve); the Samba is connected to emotions and the Vinci is connected with beauty. It's not about becoming just like a Samurai or a Samba or a Vinci, but rather a much more malleable and flexible leader who is well equipped to deal with the 21st century challenges that we're facing right now.

No matter how aware we become of our own persona and what triggers us, we are not going to change our fundamental persona after experiencing the SSV process. A Vinci will not magically transform into a Samurai, for instance; it simply takes too long to achieve that level of mastery. Rather, think of the SSV Way™ as a lens on the camera of our lives, one that allows us to zoom in on who we are and why we think and feel the way we do.

As our self-awareness grows, we gain insights about what specifically can trigger us and why we get upset or annoyed at times. What bothers a Samurai rolls right off a Vinci; what irks a Samba is no big deal for a Samurai. Nine times out of ten the cause of our annoyance can be traced to who we are being. Life becomes a bit easier, therefore, when we understand the ways the other personas influence our present behavior and show up in both our professional and personal relationships. Not only can the SSV Way™ lead us away from reactions that no longer serves us, but it also can lead us toward a future free from conflict and misunderstandings.

That's a future we can all get excited about!

PART IV: POWERING UP

Chapter 26: Personal Time and Self-Care

Imagine a computer that you never turn off. Never give it a break. Eventually it wears down and starts doing funny things. Programs don't load as quickly. The screen freezes. Strange windows open randomly and won't close no matter how many times you click the little x in the upper right-hand corner. Things can get so bad, the operating system has no other choice but to default into what's known in IT circles as "the black screen of death."

Leaders experience similar malfunctions when we don't take the time for rest, relaxation and yes, fun! Sleepless nights, bad backs, high blood pressure, weight gain, and depression are all signs telling us we need to hit the reset button of our lives and take a time out. Samurai Samba Vinci leaders work very hard, making the need for personal time and care imperative.

Personal time and self-care are not negotiable for the Samurai Samba Vinci leader. The best way to accomplish this is through a mix of activities that nurture the body, the mind and the soul. I have developed a self-care practice that includes the following parts. These work well for me; I invite you to use them as a guide to build your own self-care routine.

Body

When I was overweight, my blood pressure was high, and I was a "good" candidate for type 2 diabetes. I felt lethargic all the time and had no energy. Thankfully, I recognized I needed to make some changes.

I started nurturing my body in three ways:

a) Exercise - I started exercising, first with the New York Times Scientific 7-Minute workout and then with Shaun T's Insanity Workout. In the beginning, I felt I was going to die. I would look at my watch and see that only 5 minutes had passed. Are you kidding me? I thought as sweat stung my eyes. I stuck with it though and, over time, my body responded positively. What a different exercise can make!

b) Intermittent fasting and "healthier" eating - When I heard about all the benefits of intermittent fasting and started practicing it, coupled with eating healthier and in smaller portions, I started to see major shifts in my energy levels. There are many different types of intermittent fasting programs to choose from, but the easiest one for me to follow and stick to (due to my travels) is called "leangains," which means that I can only eat from 12pm to 8pm every day.

c) Supplements – As much as possible, I like to get most of my daily vitamins and minerals from foods I eat, but I also like to complement what I eat with high-quality supplements. Sound nutrition makes a bigger difference than many people realize – until they cut out the junk and for the first time truly feel healthy.

Mind

As brain research continues to advance our understanding of the "super computer" between our ears, we can pay greater attention to practicing good mind health habits. Meditation is one of these habits and in the next chapter, I dive deeper into its power to transform our lives and leadership capabilities.

For now, I'd like to offer a simple list of activities that are scientifically proven to improve our minds. If you recall my story from chapter seven when I was in dire financial straits, you will remember that mindfulness played an enormous role in my ability to tackle that tough time in my life. Good brain health habits you can begin or enrich right now include:

- Reading, both fiction and non-fiction
- Listening to music, books and/or podcasts
- Spending time pursuing a hobby
- Writing in a journal
- Working with your hands
- Watching a favorite movie
- Playing games
- Painting

Soul

With so many pressures coming at us from all directions in our hectic, 21st century world, we need to take extra care of our souls. One of the best ways to practice good "soul care" is through play. A pickup game of basketball, a round of table tennis or two, kickball behind the house, tossing a football or Frisbee in the park, and inviting some friends over for a Cards against Humanity tournament can leave us feeling energized, elated, and alive. As a leader, don't overlook the importance of caring for your soul. There's a reason why the saints and sages throughout millennia have encouraged us to revitalize our spirits through the power of play.

Chapter 27: Meditation

Meditation is no longer relegated to the realm of New Age practitioners assembling in mountain retreats for weekends of sitting on mats and chanting. Meditation these days is mainstream, and it fits right in with the Samurai Samba Vinci Way™. More than ever, it is a key factor in maintaining optimal brain health.

There is no one right way to meditate. I remember when I was teaching university classes in different types of meditation. In a class of 20 people, each and every one of those people had different preferences and different backgrounds.

I was teaching about five or six different meditation styles. Some of the meditation styles were a really good fit for some people, others weren't. Finding the right meditation style is important so that a) you can be consistent with it and b) you gain the many benefits meditation has to offer. You need to sample different meditation styles to see what works for you. Once you do that, you can adapt what you're learning to your life. Be sure not to merely focus on the theory of it, but also try to implement what you're learning into a practice.

Sometimes people say, "I just can't quiet my mind. It doesn't work." This can be an excuse, as if to say, "I'm not committed to doing this." More often than not, though, it is merely because they are new to the practice.

One way to begin meditating and achieving centeredness is to focus on a lit candle for a few minutes. That's one of the easiest ones to try, especially if you have never meditated before. This practice works well for all SSV personas. Another is to focus on your breath. Close your eyes and concentrate on the rhythm of your breathing. Your mind will soon calm down, and, as they say, that little mind monkey going all around inside your head will eventually surrender and say, "Oh my God, get me out of here!"

When you're focusing on your breath or when you're focusing on that candle, the constant brain chatter starts dissipating. That's when you start meditating.

You don't have to meditate for long stretches of time to reap benefits. Studies on meditation conducted at Harvard University show that only a few minutes of meditation a day can heap mountains of benefits on us including:

- Decreased anxiety
- Improved emotional stability
- Increased happiness
- Greater clarity and peace of mind
- A sharper mind with the ability to solve problems faster

Not only that, but because you are practicing daily, you become much more adaptable, much more malleable and much readier for any curveball that comes your way.

When you're working on your core through a meditation practice, anything that comes your way is doable.

Chapter 28: Taking Time off

Amystique surrounds people who work all the time in countries like America, where taking vacations is almost frowned upon. How could you be committed to your job if you are sipping umbrella drinks on the beaches of Costa Rica?

While exercise is good for the body, and meditation is good for the mind, taking some time off is good for the soul. Studies reveal that one of the secrets of top performers is that they take vacations. A Samurai Samba Vinci leader embraces time off, knowing it will only make him better at his job when he's at work.

About the value of vacations, Richard Branson says: "When you go on vacation, your routine is interrupted; the places you go and the new people you meet can inspire you in unexpected ways. As an entrepreneur or business leader, if you didn't come back from your vacation with some ideas about how to shake things up, it's time to consider making some changes."

Other Samurai Samba Vinci type leaders like Facebook's COO Sheryl Sandberg and eBay's ex-CEO John Donahue sing the praises of taking vacations. Donahue tries to take a two week vacation every year on Cape Cod with his family where he can completely disconnect from everything.

I recently traveled to Brazil for both work and pleasure, combining my visit with professional duties and some down time with my family. Tacking on two or three extra days for some R&R on the front and/or back end of a business trip can do wonders for our attitudes, not to mention bodies and souls. A change of scene, a different pace, and a new perspective even for a day or two can energize an SSV leader unlike anything else.

As Jim Moffat, Managing Principal, Deloitte Global Consulting says, "A true leader steps back, trusts his or her people, and allows them to succeed. By taking a break from the day-to-day operations, not only was I spending some much-needed time with my family, but also, I was able to focus on the bigger picture of where we were and where our business was heading. I've tried to follow this advice in my own life ever since."

Trust that your team will take care of things while you take care of yourself. The payoff for days off is often pleasantly surprising.

Chapter 29: Ongoing Assessments and Continuous Improvement

Along with taking personal time and developing a meditation practice, ongoing assessments can help the Samurai Samba Vinci leader stay sharp and play at the top of her game. Combined with the results we get from the SSV Profile Assessment, we can use the results we get from a variety of credible and effective tools, systems and techniques to help us achieve our goals.

The best assessment that I have seen so far for discovering your leadership competencies is the Leadership Circle Profile™. Developed by Robert J. Anderson, the Leadership Circle Profile™ is a comprehensive assessment that has been tested in a multitude of countries around the world, with tens of thousands of people having taken it to date. I don't have time or space to go into everything related to this assessment, but I highly encourage you to learn more about it by visiting their website at **www.leadershipcircle.com.**

For now, here are a few highlights as explained on their website:

"The Leadership Circle Profile™ is the only 360-degree

competency assessment that simultaneously provides focused competency feedback while revealing the underlying assumptions that are causing a leader's pattern of strengths and limitations. The Leadership Circle Profile™ helps leaders understand the relationship between how they habitually think, how they behave, and, more importantly, how all this impacts their current level of leadership effectiveness. Once this awareness is established, leadership development can proceed. Without it, change rarely happens."

They cover two main domains of leadership: creative competencies and reactive tendencies. The creative competencies contribute to a leader's effectiveness. According to their extensive research, creative competencies involve: Relating (caring connection, fosters team play, collaborator, mentoring and developing, interpersonal intelligence); Self-awareness (selfless leader, balance, composure, personal learner), Authenticity (integrity, courageous authenticity); Systems awareness (community concern, sustainable productivity, systems thinker); and Achieving (strategic focus, purposeful and visionary, achieves results, decisiveness).

The reactive tendencies, on the other hand, limit effectiveness, authentic expression and empowering leadership. Reactive tendencies include: Complying (conservative, pleasing, belonging, passive); Protecting (arrogance, critical, distance); and Controlling (perfect, driven, ambition and autocratic). One of my goals with clients is to use the SSV Way™ as a means of shoring up their creative competencies while minimizing their reactive ones.

Another assessment that I personally like is Gallup's

StrengthsFinder 2.0 (**http://www.strengthsfinder.com**). This assessment describes the talents that, according to author Marcus Buckingham, we should be focusing on to be successful. The first time I was introduced to this theory of focusing on our strengths, I immediately thought about the actor Jackie Chan. Did you know he still speaks in broken English, despite the numerous films he's made? Perfecting his English-speaking abilities had no bearing on his success, and in some ways, may have enhanced it!

Can you imagine if he put time and energy into becoming a flawless English speaker before making the movies that have made him a global star? Had he done that, he may never have become the Hollywood icon he is today, delighting audiences with his physical prowess, penchant for mischief and unforgettable fight scenes.

The same thought process applies to becoming a leader. Certain skills, knowledge and competencies are essential for leading confidently while others fall into the "nice to have" category with a "good enough to pass" grade. When we focus on our strengths rather than our weaknesses, we increase our chances of succeeding. Deciding to invest time and resources into ways of reinforcing what we're already good at can pay us far more dividends in the long run than spending our time in remedial-type experiences that will most likely delay our growth rather than encourage it.

The third assessment that I often use is called Kolbe A™ assessment, by Kolbe Corp (**www.kolbe.com**). This assessment addresses the instinctive way we do things. The Kolbe A™ assessment is divided into four main distinctions: Fact Finder,

Follow Thru, Quick Start and Implementor. While this is not the place for me to go into depth about this assessment, here is a brief example of two of the distinctions.

If you are a high Fact Finder like I am, for example, you will want to do as much research as you possibly can before taking action. If, on the other hand, you are a high Quick Start, you will act first and ask questions later. Can you imagine these two types trying to work together without knowing their M.O.s? Just like a Samurai and Samba working together without knowing the other's leadership style, these two different Kolbe's would get on each other's nerves quickly. The Fact Finder would feel that the Quick Start would be "rushing things" while the Quick Start would say that the Fact Finder is "overthinking everything." Awareness can go a long way in preventing most misunderstandings!

When we combine these three assessments, we have a well-rounded picture of the leader. Starting by understanding what her competencies are and what needs to be worked on and refined, we can pinpoint where her talents and strengths lie; we can also understand how she tackles any tasks she may face.

Armed with the new insights you will garner from taking various assessments, you will want to next consider adopting a multifaceted approach for continuous improvement. At minimum, you will want to stay on top of keeping your intellect sharp and well-tuned, your perspective of life keen, your body and posture strong, your executive presence regal, your moods and emotions regulated and your daily interactions with people around you friendly and conscientious.

Let's start with your intellect as this is the easiest one for subject matter experts. There are several ways for you to develop your leadership competencies.

The first is to choose what I refer to as a "low investment" option. Low investment options include things like books and online courses. On the grand continuum of long-term effectiveness, these tend to be brief compared to "high investment" options like working with a boutique consultancy, getting one-on-one coaching and developing a bespoke training program, all of which have a "high effectiveness" rating.

Let's start with books, the low investment option. Some good books on the list include:

Crucial Accountability by Kerry Patterson and Joseph Grenny is the best book I know for holding people accountable.

Be the Boss Everyone Wants to Work For by William A. Gentry Ph.D. caused an immediate change in a friend's direct report after he read it. The book helped him understand what it takes to lead people.

The One Minute Manager by Ken Blanchard offers a nice way to think about what your long-term goal is for your employees.

Mastering Leadership by Robert J. Anderson and William A. Adams shows us a fantastic leadership framework.

The Innovator's Way by Peter J. Denning and Robert Dunham provides readers with a framework for innovation as well as tools for increasing collaborative effectiveness.

The Leadership Dojo by Richard Strozzi-Heckler addresses what executive presence looks like and ways for readers to work on developing it.

Presence by Peter Senge et. al. provides insights about how we can become change agents within our organizations.

Coaching to the Human Soul Volumes I & II by Alan Sieler can help managers who want to become coach-managers and/or coach-leaders discover what's necessary to do that.

After books, I would say that online courses are the second least expensive option. Two good options include:

Udemy **(www.udemy.com)** – search for "leadership development"

Harvard ManageMentor **(http://harvardbusiness.org/harvard-managementor)**

A third option on the scale of the least to the most expensive would be open-enrollment trainings. Some examples are:

Situational leadership II (Ken Blanchard) - **www.kenblanchard.com**

"Exercising Influence" from Barnes & Conti - **www.barnesconti.com**

The fourth option would be boutique consultancies which can provide customized solutions by seasoned professionals who have been delivering this type of work for 15, 20 and even 25 years. My company Toyama&Co offers customized leadership development solutions for both individuals and organizations – **www.toyamaco.com**

The fifth option would be big consultancies that have a leadership development arm that can provide these types of services all around the world.

The sixth option would be to hire a boutique consultancy

that can help your company set up your own branded university. For example, say you work for Acme company. A boutique consultancy that specializes in setting up a university branded to your company would create "Acme University," with the courses delivered by the boutique consultancy using professionals who have decades of experience on the subjects your company would like to train your staff, but at a fraction of the cost of setting up your own university and running it internally.

Chapter 30: Support and Accountability

No one who has succeeded in life has done it without the help of a coach or a mentor. We see professionals in many arenas today who claim they wouldn't be where they are had it not been for the help they got from a person or group who held them accountable for getting things done. I've certainly reaped the rewards afforded by working with coaches.

Success cannot happen in a vacuum. The Samurai Samba Vinci leader knows this, and seeks counsel from trusted advisors. Eventually, you will want to consider joining a community of like-minded people who are committed to their own leadership success -- and yours. That's why I created programs where you can get deeper training not only in the SSV Way™, but also where you can meet other like-minded people who are ramping up their leadership skills.

Something that catches newly promoted subject matter experts off guard is how much their circle of influence changes once they are in their new position. Whereas they once worked side by side with other engineers in their company, for example, now they are leading them. The relationship dynamic changes, as do the problems.

It's important to find people who understand what it's like to be in your new position when seeking answers to work-related problems. As much as you may love grabbing a beer with your former work team, their day-to-day experiences are no longer the same as yours. I'm not suggesting you can longer be friends with former SME colleagues; I am recommending you seek out confidantes who are either currently in a similar position or are one or two levels above where you are now. To find people who hold you accountable in the best possible way and explore the SSV community, visit **www.toyamaco.com/ssvbook**

The Internet is full of excellent resources. A quick Google search using the keywords "leadership mastermind" and "how to start a book group at work" yield millions of results. Here are some popular ways to find the support and accountability you will need in your new leadership role:

Masterminds

I won't lie – the SSV Mastermind is exceptional (you can learn more about it at **www.toyamaco.com/ssvbook**). However, you may want to ultimately form your own mastermind within the parameters of your company, or to match specific goals you've set for yourself. I've taken part in several high-level masterminds over the years and can say confidently that they've played a significant role in my own progress as a leader.

Facebook Groups

With close to 2 billion users as of the writing of this book, Facebook is where people spend time. An hour or so of searching for groups related to leadership on Facebook can yield plenty of options from which to choose. Some groups are open, while others are closed and require administrative approval to belong. A quick way to get started is to search for a public leader you like by name and then like his or her page. For example, Bill Gates has a public Facebook page anyone can like. You can learn from posts in the newsfeed as well as meet people virtually who may share your views on leadership.

Online Forums

Online forums such as Reddit **(www.reddit.com)** and Quora **(www.quora.com)** can offer decent answers to common questions about every topic under the sun, including leadership.

Internal Employee Groups

Many companies have internal groups where employees can meet up for informal and formal get togethers. These groups might be arranged by department, title, gender, or common interest. Forming cross-departmental alliances could play in your favor as you hone your leadership skills.

Book Groups

I have a realtor friend who belongs to a book group within her company. Each month, the group chooses a non-fiction book that will foster personal and professional growth for everyone in the group. They meet for an hour each month on site to discuss the book and then select the following month's read. A book group like this may already exist at your organization; if not, you might consider starting one!

Local Meetups

Meet ups have gained traction in the last few years. A quick search on **www.meetup.com** will list for you multiple groups within your region. Categorized by theme or topic, these groups can connect you with people who share a common interest. Everything from microbrews to belly dancing exists.

Remember: sometimes our best professional connections form when we are engaged in a non-work-related activity.

LinkedIn Groups

For connecting with professionals who share your interests, philosophies and aspirations, LinkedIn groups can't be beat. Some groups are open while others require an invitation or administrative approval to join. Use the search bar inside LinkedIn with keywords related to your interests to discover groups. You can also do a cross-search for groups via connections you already have and request an invitation to join a group of particular interest. Once a part of a group, you can join the conversation, network and learn from existing members. Use common sense and post things that have intrinsic value to many so you gain a reputation as a thought leader rather than someone who merely wants to promote an agenda. When approached thoughtfully, LinkedIn groups can open doors in unimagined and exciting ways!

CONCLUSION

At the time of this writing, my daughter is 18 months old. One of the beauties of her age is that she doesn't know yet what it means to feel inadequate. In many ways, I want her to never feel "less than." Not that I want her to live in a bubble; put simply, I want her to have such an unwavering core (Samurai) that she does not get fazed by negative comments. I also want her to feel free to express herself through new ideas (Vinci) while remaining open to the natural rhythms of life (Samba).

Can you imagine what the world would look like if every human being felt whole and complete? What would the creative process be like if it came from feeling as if we are a manifestation of Source?

We live in a world where people want templates and checklists for quick assessments. "Give me the boxes that I can check off so I can get on to the next thing" is a prevailing attitude. But just like a master chef's signature dish at a five-star restaurant doesn't follow a recipe on the label of a soup can, leadership can't be hastily scratched into bullet points on the back of a cocktail napkin.

When I look back at many so called "bad" bosses I've encountered, a sheer number of them were "bad" because they had deep, core wounds that made them feel inadequate, not because they were incompetent. When we feel inadequate, we feel the need to overcompensate for that inadequacy. That urge can either manifest in creation or destruction. It can be a creative force if we strive to improve ourselves; it can be a destructive force if we blame others for our feelings of inadequacy.

In a competitive and fierce global economy, companies need to make a profit to survive. I understand this. But in many cases, we have gone too far in one direction: making money at any cost, no matter the consequences.

In some ways, we have lost the essence of why we even exist.

Imagine for a minute what it would feel like to work in a harmonious company: a company where people communicate what they mean, where unintentional backstabbing and "bad politics" don't exist, and where everyone is treated like a human being rather than just a "resource" to be discarded whenever they are no longer productive. Imagine companies where Samurai Samba Vinci leaders abound, bringing forth the best in each other -- and themselves.

For anyone who works for a company that isn't like this, we may feel empty after a day's work. How many of us go to work and are "not allowed" to be the best that we can be, either because we have bad bosses or because the company structure is so stifling? Or even because we feel that our voices won't be heard?

Places like this don't have to live in our imagination, however, and can, in fact, become a reality. As we move deeper into the 21st century, we can apply the principles the Samurai Samba Vinci Way™ to assist all of us in becoming better at being our best selves. I like to think of this as what leadership expert Skip Prichard refers to as "self-mastery."

Leadership development is one of the biggest challenges facing organizations today, particularly for organizations that promote their internal subject matter experts to management positions. In my work over the last 26 years with companies in 113 countries, I have witnessed this crisis first-hand. In more cases than not, people don't want change. They simply don't like it.

But change is inevitable, and nothing new. It happens faster these days than at any other time in our history. I know change first-hand as I've moved to five different countries during my life and each time I landed in a new country, I had to learn the respective nuances of each to survive. On a certain level, I like change and even seek it out.

When cars came along at the turn of the 20th century, people resisted them. Many were unwilling to give up what was familiar -- the horse and buggy. But can you even imagine what life would be like if we still used buggies and horses?

We see signs of the future everywhere these days. Driverless cars are coming. A lot of people are resisting them. Artificial intelligence is here, too, and it's automating all kinds of tasks and processes once relegated to humans only. Consensus is building around the notion that the jobs our children will have as adults haven't even been invented yet. The world my daughter is growing up in is completely different than the world I grew up in. Really different.

Thankfully, we humans have a decent track record of adapting. We resist change at first because it's uncomfortable. Sometimes we miss great opportunities because we can be slow to come around to an idea. How many people can you think of who wished they'd seen Google before it became Google? I know I sure do!

Given what's on the near horizon, the need for new leaders is here, and it's urgent. The world is ready to embrace a new leadership model like the Samurai Samba Vinci Way™, one that teaches people how to be in touch with their core values, who are flexible in different situations, and who meet challenges about the future with creative thinking and a spirit of possibility. The world needs leaders who bring the different parts of themselves to everything they do, rather than living in one world at home and in a different world at work.

Leadership development is an ongoing process. Not every tool that got you where you are today will get you where you need to go tomorrow. The Samurai Samba Vinci Way™ can guide you on that journey. Some readers will get exactly what you need from reading this book alone. Others of you may be looking for some extra guidance and want to team up with experts who can take you through a customized experience interacting with the concepts I've presented in this book.

I invite you to take a deeper look at how the principles I've shared with you in this book can assist you on your leadership journey. To discover what that can look like, please visit **www. toyamaco.com/ssvbook**

APPENDIX

The following chart provides some key characteristics of each persona. As you look over this table, think about which words resonate with you most at your core. Circle the top 5-10 words that ring mosta true for you on instinct.

Samurai (Japan)	Samba (Brazil)	Vinci (Italy)
Perfection	Chaos	Creativity
Precision	Flow	Innovation
Technique	Improvisation	Beauty
Mastery	Fun	Appreciation
Seriousness	Fluidity	Sense of exploration
Discipline	"In the moment"	
Rigidity	Flexible	Has both Formal and Informal elements
Functionality	Receptive to failure and making mistakes	
Formality		Cross-pollination of different areas of expertise (like the Renaissance-- the meeting of the minds made that time so creative. Blending ideas to create new things. Surgeon meeting with an artist meeting with an astro-physicist) (How I can mix things to make something new and more beautiful?)
Intellectual	Informal	
Continuous improvement (How can I make this better with either less effort or less time?)	Emotional	
	Expressive	
	Playful	

Samurai (Japan)	Samba (Brazil)	Vinci (Italy)
Sushi, Sweets, Tea Ceremonies - all done with perfection Gray, silver, brown, black -- colder, harder colors	Yellow, orange, raspberry, turquoise, lime green, ribbons flowing	Rich jewel tones like violet, forest green, burgundy, royal blue, all with gold around the edges

7 ESSENTIAL CHARACTERISTICS OF 21ST CENTURY LEADERSHIP

Not too long ago, I was invited to speak at West Point about 21st century leadership. The following seven essential characteristics of 21st century leadership come from the presentation I made there.

1. Connection and Care

Connection and care are key to leadership. You may have heard about how empathy is crucial to being a good leader. But how do you connect with someone who has completely opposite views from you? Understanding from where they are coming is a first step. Are you aware of the life story that is driving their actions? We need to remember that we are all human beings. We are not machines and very few people on this planet hurt others on purpose. We are driven by emotions (even though we love to think that what drives us is logic – this couldn't be further from the truth) as proven over and over again by neuroscience studies.

For instance, we have all found ourselves saying, "This is not the right time to be having this conversation." We know that we are in a closed off emotional state and highly charged; we might be angry, sad, frustrated, or even hungry.

We know that when we are in a different emotional state, we can handle the difficult conversation better. It isn't the subject matter that changes, it's the emotional state when discussing the subject matter.

Tip: One of the quickest changes a leader can make to increase productivity is by creating a climate of neutrality where emotions are calm and conversations can be conducted effectively. Learning that the right conversation in the wrong emotional state is the wrong conversation can alter the way an entire office does business.

2. Knowledge and Wisdom

Successful leaders have a solid knowledge base. What distinguishes the more successful from the less successful is the wisdom they show in the face of adversity. It's not enough to simply "know" information. The best leaders embody their knowledge through mindful practices that incorporate their fair share of recurrence. This ensures that they can access it whenever needed.

One example of the way I help my clients embody knowledge is with presentation training. I have them practice the same presentation repeatedly with a focus on a different element each time (i.e. content, intonation, voice projection, posture, gestures, flow, etc.)

Tip: The next time you are assigned to present material, try this exercise. Run through your presentation 3-5 times, switching just your speaking accent each time you make it.

If you are a native Spanish speaker, try speaking with a British, American, and Chinese accent. You can also use volume: Run through your presentation shouting, whispering, and changing back and forth between shouting and whispering. Make notes about how each one feels, and how each one affected your understanding of the material.

3. Presence

Strong leaders have a strong presence. In turbulent times, leaders who practice presence are resilient and still seize the occasion. This is how strong leaders exude their strength. Their presence is felt even when they are going through tough times.

Leaders do the daily work needed, like meditation, to stabilize their presence, bring their presence, align it with their purpose, and remain strong even during challenging circumstances. If that work is not done and reinforced on a daily basis, it becomes too easily pulled in different directions when times get tough.

Tip: There are many different ways to meditate, so choose the one that aligns with your schedule and mood.

4. Systems Thinking & Making a Difference

When I gave one of my talks at West Point's cemetery, I thought about the leaders who fought for a cause they believed in. This was an emotional and powerful experience for me as I reflected on those that came before me. I couldn't help but think about what difference I am making in my life now and what impact I will leave behind when I am gone.

Tip: Take a few minutes and ask yourself the following questions:

- What will the ripple effects be tomorrow of decisions you make today?
- Will your actions be admired/applauded when you are no longer active in your current role or when you are long gone?

- Will you have left a positive impact on the world?
- What will be the impact of your actions now, and in 10, 20, 30 years' time?
- On any given day, for any given project or event, how will what you are about to do impact others around you?

I realize it can be difficult to project what your life could be like many years from now, but great leaders practice this skill often so that asking themselves these questions becomes second nature -- and their decision-making skills are rock solid.

5. Innovation

Successful leaders are always trying to find new ways to innovate. It's not about chasing the newest, shiniest object. It's about building a strong foundation with the products and services that you currently offer, then making sure you continue to innovate.

Most of us in the business world have heard of the Apple II and the Macintosh divisions at Apple. The Apple II was the cash cow and the Macintosh division was the innovative one.

Steve Jobs built a strong financial foundation that he could use as a stepping stone for building new and innovative products. Leaders that are innovative follow a system to be effective. A system I personally recommend is "Eight Practices" found in the book The Innovator's Way - by Peter Denning and Bob Dunham.

Tip: Do a quick "innovation inventory" of your current role and place of business. What systems and processes could use some fresh ideas? What's working well as it is right now?

6. Humility

Some of the most impactful leaders that I met at West Point were both humble yet highly successful at the same time (many of them were multi-millionaires). This wasn't the first time I found this combination to be true.

I remember when I was going through graduate school in business administration in Brazil. I had the opportunity to meet some of the most successful businessmen in the country. So many of them were incredibly down to earth, genuine, humble, and left their mark everywhere they went. The connection between humility and success was blatant.

It isn't one to overlook.

7. Passion

Leaders who stood out at West Point had a burning desire to make a positive impact. Their passion for their subject matter was palpable. Are you passionate about what you do? If not, what would it take for you to become passionate about your work?

Tip: Ask yourself, "What are you passionate about? How can you incorporate your passions into your current work?"

NEXT STEPS

As you can see from this list, six out of the seven traits of successful leaders are related to whom they are being as people, not only what information they possess. Which of the seven traits are your strongest? Do you consider yourself to be masterful at any? Which ones will you commit to building within yourself?

Great leadership in the 21st century lives at the intersection of these three main personas -- Samurai, Samba and Vinci. When combined, they present a powerful framework for personal and professional growth across all industries.

IN THE MEDIA

USA [in English]

TV

The 3 Biggest Mistakes Women Make When Rising to the Top and How to Avoid Them

- NBC New Mexico - Good Day New Mexico (KOB) **https://vimeo.com/218301394**
- FOX New Mexico - New Mexico Living (KRQE) **https://vimeo.com/217294337**

Forbes.com

Seven Leadership Insights From West Point

- **https://www.forbes.com/sites/forbescoachescouncil/2017/02/28/seven-leadership-insights-from-west-point/**

If You Want Your Employees to Master Their Craft, Focus on Your Culture

- **https://www.forbes.com/sites/forbescoachescouncil/2016/08/31/if-you-want-your-employees-to-master-their-craft-focus-on-your-culture/**

Podcast

Claudio Toyama Aims for Mastery & Strives for Excellence

- Play Your Position Podcast **http://playyourpositionpodcast.com/claudio/**

West Point -Leadership Speakers Academy

- Leadership the Samurai Samba Vinci Way™ - **https://vimeo.com/187898807**

Brazil [in Portuguese]

Newspaper Folha de Sao Paulo

Executivos 'fora da curva' ganham até 144% a mais – expert quote

- http://www1.folha.uol.com.br/sobretudo/carreiras/ 2017/06/1891885-executivos-fora-da-curva-ganham-ate-144-a-mais.shtml

HSM Update - Quando a sua empresa vai parar de imitar as outras? http://www.distefanoconsultoria.com/artigoshsm/ Quandoasuaempresavaiparardeimitarasoutras.pdf

For a more comprehensive list of Media appearances, please visit: http://www.toyamaco.com/media-appearances/

BIBLIOGRAPHY

Charan, Ram. (2011). *The Leadership Pipeline: How to Build the Leadership Powered Company.* Jossy-Bass.

Denning, Peter and Bob Dunham. (2010). *The Innovator's Way: Essential Practices for Successful Innovation.* The MIT Press.

Deutschendorf, Harvey. (June 22, 2015). "Why Emotionally Intelligent People Are More Successful." FAST Company. **https://www.fastcompany.com/3047455/why-emotionally-intelligent-people-are-more-successful**

Feltman, Charles. (2008). *The Thin Book of Trust: An Essential Primer for Building Trust at Work.* Thin Book Publishing.

Jensen, Rolf and Mika Aaltonen. (2013). *The Renaissance Society: How the Shift from Dream Society to the Age of Individual Control Will Change the Way You Do Business.* McGraw-Hill Education.

Kiger, David. (December 24, 2016). "CEOs and the Importance of Taking Vacation Time." Business 2 Community. **http://www.business2community.com/leadership/ceos-importance-taking-vacation-time-01743501#f1BYZ9lbEJc6ZOe3.99**

Morin, Kate. (June 10, 2017). "5 Intermittent Fasting Methods: Which One Is Right for You?" Daily Burn. **http://dailyburn.com/life/health/intermittent-fasting-methods/**

Olivero, Gerald, K. Denise Bane and Richard E. Kopelman. (December 1, 1997). "Executive Coaching as a Transfer of Training Tool: Effects on Productivity in a Public Agency." Sage Journals. **http://journals.sagepub.com/doi/abs/10.1177/009102609702600403**

O' Leonard, Karen and Laci (Barb) Loew. (July 16, 2012). "Leadership Development Factbook 2012: Benchmarks and Trends in U.S. Leadership Development." **http://www.bersin.com/Store/ details.aspx?docid=15587**

Rampton, John. (January 25, 2016). "How Richard Branson and Other Leaders Take Time Off." Inc Magazine. **https://www.inc. com/john-rampton/how-much-time-average-ceo-s-take- off-every-year.html**

Reynolds, Gretchen. (May 9, 2013). "The Scientific 7-Minute Workout." The New York Times. **https://well.blogs. nytimes.com/2013/05/09/the-scientific-7-minute- workout/?mcubz=1&_r=0**

Stipp, David. (January 1, 2013). "How Intermittent Fasting Might Help You Live a Longer and Healthier Life." Scientific American. **https://www.scientificamerican.com/article/ how-intermittent-fasting-might-help-you-live-longer- healthier-life/**

Strock, James M. (2010). *Serve to Lead: Your Transformational 21st Century Leadership System.* Serve to Lead Press.

ABOUT THE AUTHOR

Award-winning speaker Claudio Toyama is the CEO of Toyama&Co., an International leadership consultancy specializing in building sustainable peak performance cultures. He has delivered projects in 113 countries, has travelled to over 40 of them and has lived in five different countries on four continents. Claudio's ability to create paradigm shifts in corporate culture results in more thoughtful leadership, a staff of brand ambassadors and customers who feel the difference and embrace it. He is the co-author of Leadership: The Faculty of Leadership Speakers Academy at West Point, a Forbes contributor, and is a featured guest on TV, including NBC and FOX. He lives with his daughter outside Washington, DC (USA). Meet Claudio at **www.toyamaco.com**